MW00697901

Your Children Are Boring

Your Children Are Boring

Or
How Modern Parents Ruin Everything

Tom James

Published by Sauce Materials
Copyright © 2020 Tom James
The moral right of the author has been asserted.

No part of this book may be copied, stored in a retrieval system, or reproduced in any format, by any means, electronic or otherwise, without the express permission of the copyright owner and publisher.

ISBN-10: 1712629972
ISBN-13: 978-1712629970

Cover design www.StudioDelme.com

@TomJayAuthor

www.tomjameswriting.com

www.saucematerials.co.uk

For Mum

Table of Contents

Introduction   ix

What's Going On?   1
The Rod Hull Syndrome   11
Spatial Awareness   15
Join Us...   19
Your House Is a Mess   25
They're Not Special   29
Who Are You?   33
Ooh Look at Me   37
You're So Boring   41
It Doesn't Make You Less Selfish   47
You're a Big Child Too   57
This Won't End Well   63

Acknowledgements   77
References   79

Introduction

Virtue is the golden mean between two vices,
the one of excess and the other of deficiency.

Aristotle

WHILE IT'S TEMPTING to write 'I do not hate children! I do not hate children!' repeatedly in this introduction, there's little point as it's the inevitable conclusion that some parents will reach if they read this book, clutching at their papoose straps angrily.

Even attempting to question the prevalent culture of child worship is treated as the embittered ranting of a nihilist, and it's exactly that sort of blind arrogance that should be wrestled with.

Society's increasing obsession with children is embedded deeper than a tick in Kim Philby's back, but more and more voices are trying to pull at the reins of this runaway horse.

Why have so many parents decided that their child is the most important object ever created when there is such strong evidence to believe the opposite is true?

It's terribly unlikely that *your* little Jackson or Jemima, Sylvia or Stanley, Parker or Prudence, will be the most interesting, unique, and endlessly fascinating human on Earth. Oh and creative, they're all creative aren't they. If one was to believe every parent's claim about his or her children, we're going to end up with a whole generation of Picassos or Sartres in about twenty years, ushering in a new renaissance. Or they're intellectual powerhouses because they answered a question correctly on a TV quiz and now they're part of a movement that is a new age of enlightenment.

And they're not in good company by the way; Violet Kray was terribly proud of her boys. Her 'little princes' were the apples of her eye, they were mummy's little miracles; and they couldn't do a thing wrong.

Where was this outlook when these parents were child-free by the way, let alone single? I don't recall endless conversations with my friends about how interesting children were or that they didn't think they were complete until they'd had children, or they wouldn't be a real person until they'd experienced being a mum / dad. A sort of convenient amnesia affects some people once they have kids. It's almost as if this shit has been invented to needlessly justify their decisions.

For example, a particular radio presenter in the United Kingdom demonstrates the typical moral flexibility at play here. This person, like so many of the dads of his age and class, was the archetypal 1990s man; unconvincingly adopting the cultural attire and jokey misogyny of new ladism after watching Britpop videos and realising that cor blimey could be cool, he adjusted his public school tones to drop consonants like a Blair-era politician and an accompanying healthy distrust of religion.

He'll call anyone with a regional accent, especially a London one, 'mate' and effect riotous yet somehow nervous laughter when anyone from an ethnic minority calls in as he ham-fistedly attempts to ingratiate himself with the proles (of course, only up to the point that they say something in support of Brexit).

The required boxes ticked, and like many a Gen-Xer, he and his partner had a baby. A daughter and his transformation began. All of a sudden, virtually everything he discussed was done through the prism of *his* parenthood; his views changed (as many people's do) but with a gusto and newfound intolerance of anyone who disagreed with this life choice.

Settling down with his wife and kid also meant he 'became reli-gious', a shift one could logically (if cynically) attribute more to the act of finding a better school for his kid than some kind of existential realisation.

He turned his entire moral standing on radio into something backed up by being a parent and how it 'just makes you see things differently' (and by differently he means, in a better and more com-passionate way. In a wiser, more considered way than those without children.). Sound familiar?

That's right, it's not that his behaviour is remarkable, it's all too common. And while he is a particularly loathsome example, one won-ders how such individuals are able to hold themselves in high esteem morally while simultaneously demonstrating an ability to drop their opinionated stances and alter their views based purely on their own personal choices and circumstances.

It's the reasonable, grown-up, thoughtful parents that you don't notice. Or at least, you don't notice *that* they're parents. They're not pushing you into the road with their buggy while they look at their phone. They're not posting online that having a child has made them less selfish. They wouldn't dream of explaining to you that *their* child is actually really special while you are forced to stare at yet another incoherent daubing. And they don't bore you with the same repeti-tive tale of how tiring it is.

This book tries to address how this has manifested itself in the mod-ern world – a bit. Why it has come to define some, why it has turned many parents into insufferable bores, and why have they lost their awareness of other people? But mostly, this is a massive moan. Mostly.

This isn't a push to retreat to the 1950s where you'd get a clip round the ear if you were lucky, a nasty case of rickets, and you called men Sir or Mister (though I do actually like that last one).

The alternative doesn't have to be children hiding at the top of the stairs, peering through the bannisters while Mama and Papa entertain the local vicar, knowing not to speak until spoken to or face a harsh 'talking to' from father's hefty walking stick.

It's not a nostalgia trip either. Plenty of things weren't as good in the olden days – there was polio in swimming pools, scurvy, and of course, *Tickle on the Tum*.

Take a trip to YouTube and watch some adverts from the 1980s, or 1970s or 1960s, a time when people with tattoos were old lags or sailors rather than well everyone. Aside from the polite yet outrageous and overt sexism (and a paedophile talking about road safety) the difference in tone regarding children is marked.

Kids rarely took centre stage, unless the ad was about Action Man. They were part of a family, rather than some wise little owl that knows better than mum and dad (especially dad. Stupid dad!).

There are libraries worth of books devoted to parenting skills, why it's so hard to be a parent, how to tell if your child is a genius / on the spectrum / transgender etc., and, as if that's not enough, every parent continues to think their perspective and experience of raising children is so unique that they simply must share it with the world via their feeble blog posts.

And then there are the photos. Oh God, the photos. They go on forever, they never stop, and there appear to be very few boundaries around what these poor kids can be photographed doing. It's quite clear these parents have forgotten what sort of a person they were before they had children.

Why else would *Supernanny* (starring Jo Frost) have to keep reminding numerous idiots that it's important to spend time together without their children or that you need to have some boundaries and discipline? What sort of an imbecile needs to be reminded of things like that?

Then there are the myths of happiness and intelligence and its relationship to having children. A trope regularly trotted out by some extremely unsavoury internet-based characters who appear to want a return to more 'traditional' values where a woman's job is to breed and shut up, while almost everywhere, the most educated women are least likely to have children.

A study by two demographers, Rachel Margolis and Mikko Myrskyla, suggests that, once you control things like wealth and marital status, liberal Anglo-Saxon middle-aged child-free people appear to be happier than parents.[1] The same demographers find that young parents are gloomier than child-free youngsters. That's not to say you will be happier without kids, but perhaps the view that you can't be happy without them might need to take a flying fuck at itself?

So for the last time, to state the obvious, this isn't every parent out there. Most are able to strike a sensible balance between bringing up children in a way that doesn't expect society to be constantly nodding in agreement with them and saying 'Awwww' on demand.

As for the claim that only people who are parents can talk *about* parenting, that's a little like telling a doctor that unless he or she has had cancer, they can't treat yours.

There have always been annoying parents, and there have always been remarkable kids. And also unremarkable ones. This particularly obsessive madness is a modern phenomenon. This book isn't attacking those of you who are proud of your children, who think that he or she is the most wonderful bag of joy. That's a nice thing and hopefully comes naturally to you, and with a healthy amount of reality.

But raising a child isn't easy you know!

It's not meant to be easy! Nothing worthwhile ever is. All the same you're not decommissioning landmines every day; just try keeping them away from bleach and teaching them to say 'please', 'thank you' and 'after you'. Oh and can you stop them from staring? Didn't that used to be rude? More on that later...

It's not just the child-free who are sick of this. Go to Mumsnet and you will hear the voices of parents bemoaning that they 'can't bear to read another article about parenting'.

This is Mumsnet; it's full of parents. Clue's in the name. A more or less gentle and thoroughly useful resource that is so polite; its best-known acronym is the apologetic AIBU (which stands for 'Am I Being Unreasonable?').

Still, there's also a healthy dose of interest in and even envy of child-free people and consideration for how frustrating it must be from some Mumsnet members.

There's no need to enlarge the chasm between parents and the child-free with the two sides lobbing foul-mouthed insults from one direction and passive-aggressive, patronising platitudes from the other.

As with all things that go un-discussed, or are considered 'off limits', in polite society or the media, the first reaction is the most violent. An explosion of sorts ensues as an outpouring of pent-up frustration and undisclosed fury spew onto social media and forums.

If you really want something constructive to come from it however, alliances must be built, common ground should be found, and conversations might begin. Despite the title of this book, the aim isn't to create a schism.

If you're child-free and angry at how the wonder of parenting is rammed down your throat, there's every chance you'll find an ally in one of your friends who has kids. Many will agree with you, and at least be sympathetic. And some may even be mortified if they suspect they've contributed to it.

Most of the parents I personally know even *wait* to be asked about their kids before talking about them, and when they do it's with a measured tone, fully aware that theirs is not the only child on the planet, nor the first to get an A in school or do one of those abominable pictures, you insist on putting on your wall, of a whale / pig / mummy and daddy / insect with eleven legs (they all look the same by the way).

The rest of you though, in short, need to take a long hard look at yourself. And if you put 'Dad' or 'Mum' in your social media bios, this book is aimed at you.

Oh, and tidy your house. It's a mess.

What's Going On?

I'm thinking of something very audacious for which I'll become super unpopular. I'm thinking of instituting an award for all those young women who are healthy, who are capable of having a child, but choose not to have one.

Sadhguru

IF IT'S NOT TV programmes spying on five-year-olds to see what they get up to (and guess what, it's exactly what you expect – they run around, speak gibberish, say adorable things, lie, make up stuff to have fun, punch the weaker ones, steal things and deny when they have, and blame everyone else for everything), then it's virtually every single advertisement out there.

Adverts portray kids as these knowing, Disneyfied brats, and parents (invariably the dads) as hapless, resigned idiots who are at their child's beck and call. Oh no, dad's not at all cool but is trying to be, cue eye-rolling precocious brat who seems to have the self-awareness and worldly cynicism of some 1980s movie teenager.

The internet hasn't resisted the obsession either, despite our fascination with cats. Many parents have forgone their own identity in favour of representing themselves as their child. Every perceived mundane moment, every drawing, every dinner time, every party and every perceived, empty 'achievement' is plastered on their 'walls' and replaces *their* face on *their* profile. It's like being surrounded by the most tedious slide show in history. In fact, it *is* the most tedious slide show in history.

One doesn't want to admonish every parent who posts a picture of his or her kid on Facebook, but as with all things social it's interesting to transpose the activity to the real world. Imagine you, as one of these parents, turning up at your friend's house and immediately shoving an album of photos under their nose. Then start verbally cataloguing all the 'amusing anecdotes' your child has given you, or those funny things he or she has said. It wouldn't be long before your friend feigned a stroke and lay there until you left.

Then there's the social media phenomenon of 'virtue signalling'. Oh yes, one hears the cry, 'But virtue signalling is just another term for being nice; if that's a crime then yes, I am a virtue signaller.'

Except that it isn't that, and you know it isn't. What's more, as sure as all adverts and coffee shops are piping out music from singers who insist on doing covers in the style of a tired and depressed teenager, it tends to be those most guilty that defend virtue signalling so heartily. All signal, no virtue.

It is of course a phenomenon that is not at all exclusive to parents. Seemingly huge swathes of the globe are inflicting this particular brand of face-stroking, mirror-gazing, and self-promotion on each other. It's where competition meets a kind of censorship: I do this thing that is good; therefore, you be nice (by which I mean, don't disagree with me and don't feel free to air your views if they differ from mine or face the ultimate shame of being termed a negative Nancy or indeed, a hater or a troll).

As Nick Cohen put it, 'No good deed goes unpublicised.'[2] This must be your motto from now on.'

And kids are a handy little tool you can use to get your latest view across, or maybe just to let everyone know how caring you really are. In a tweet in 2017 Amelia Womack, the deputy leader of the UK Green Party, tweeted that her eleven-year-old nephew just said, 'He doesn't like the cover of a James Bond book with a naked woman on and he didn't think that women's bodies should be used to sell things #proudauntiemoment.'

Think about that for a moment. Imagine the nephew did say that; now, that is a stretch in all honesty. The most common response to her tweet was the staple 'Did not happen' (reassuringly, she won the 2017 Did Not Happen of the Year Award, well done, internet) – he was probably parroting things he's heard from her. But also, and this is the important part so pay attention, why tell us?

Using children as political props comes alongside huge numbers of misinformed parents who are 'fighting back!' against often imaginary forces that are apparently trying to destroy their child's future. I support this because they are 'muh children'.

As the crack-addled, bath disaster and terrible parent Whitney Houston sang, children ARE the future and every cause is made more 'powerful' if it is connected to children. On some motorways in the United Kingdom, we are told to be careful because some cherub's 'daddy' works on this stretch of road. It seems certain that the bright sparks at the Ministry of Transport saw a massive decline in deaths on the motorway once all the drivers realised that some of the workers had children.

Spare a thought then for the child-free dads working on that stretch of motorway. They were fair game. Mow those fuckers down all you like say HM Government.

And then there are the celebrities. They hit their midthirties or later, they've had a couple of spells in rehab for drugs, alcohol, sex addictions or whatever, and with their career and first marriage firmly in the toilet, they marry again, have a child and all of a sudden we need to be lectured by these blank, self-obsessed show-offs on how amazing it is being a parent. Oh and drugs are bad.

There is a stigma attached to couples that don't have children, a fascination (particularly towards women) and a suspicion of selfishness or coldness. A Mumsnet member recently posted referring to women that are child-free as 'unmilked cows'. It's somehow more wretched to see rampant misogyny coming from a mother.

To some, parenthood allegedly 'gives you perspective' and a different (let's face it, better) set of values. But what sort of person needs a child to give them perspective? It could be argued exactly the sort of person who should think twice about having one.

I once overheard a man sitting near me say, on receiving a news alert regarding the conflict on Syria, to the person next to him, 'Oh, Syria. Every time I watch something about Syria I cry. I think it's just since I had kids, stuff like that really affects me.'

Turn that on its head and you basically have a man who, when he was child-free would be stony-faced when watching the images of the tiny corpses of innocent children in some war-torn region.

Maybe he'd just sigh in the past or tut. What a lovely fella, a stand-up citizen of the world, immune to all the pain and misery. As much depth as a puddle and then BOOM! Abraca-fucking-dabra he's hit by the feely stick and becomes a well of empathy able to teach us all how to emote.

I started to wonder, do you just cry because you imagine your own children? Is it just dead children that make you cry? You don't mind so much if it's an old person? Maybe an animal?

I don't buy it and neither should you.

If you think that having a child will give you perspective; why not start a little smaller? Perhaps get a houseplant, or adopt an animal? And if all else fails, why not explore human adoption? But no, it has to have your 'genes', doesn't it? It has to have the genes of the sort of self-obsessed, detestable foghorn who needs to inflict their own particular brand of dissatisfied misery on another poor innocent being just so everyone can comment on how it looks like you and you can bask in your reimagined depth.

Some couples who left it late to have a child while they built careers spend thousands and thousands on artificial insemination on the off-chance it'll have mum's curly hair, dad's eyes, or nan's sense of humour, but it might just end up with granddad's propensity for gout and early onset male pattern baldness.

The photographer Mary Ellen Mark said of children, 'I didn't want to have them if I couldn't provide a great, nurturing home life. So I put all the energy of raising a child into my work.' And not that it should matter, but Mark is renowned for photographing children who have had difficult beginnings or suffered in some way.

The seductive untruth that parenthood provides your life with meaning and that until you do that you will aimlessly wander through life unable to find an existential anchor could of course lead to huge, life-crushing disappointment and a cruel quantity of expectation heaped on the child.

I would suggest that to dispel this myth, simply open your eyes and look around you. Many parents are the worst possible advert for this way of thinking.

For starters, here's an objectively compiled list of people who have had children:

- Saddam Hussein
- Fred and Rosemary West
- Klaus Barbie
- Henry VIII
- Mao Zedong
- Josef Stalin
- Pol Pot
- Ayatollah Khomeini
- Benito Mussolini
- Vlad the Impaler
- Osama bin Laden
- Idi Amin
- Reinhard Heydrich
- Josef Mengele
- Harold Shipman
- Kim Jong-Il
- John Wayne Gacy
- The Queen
- Heinrich Himmler
- Leopold II of Belgium
- Andrei Chikatilo

- Attila the Hun
- Dr H. H. Holmes
- Ivan the Terrible
- Genghis Khan
- Emperor Hirohito
- Muammar al-Gaddafi
- Jim Jones
- Adolf Eichmann
- Simon Cowell

And just to keep things fair, here's a random list of people who chose to be child-free:

- Émile Zola
- Christopher Walken
- Jane Austen
- Louis Armstrong
- Francis Bacon
- Lemony Snicket
- George Bernard Shaw
- Samuel Beckett
- Walt Whitman
- Pat Coombs
- Lily Tomlin
- Ludwig van Beethoven
- Oprah Winfrey
- Siouxsie Sioux
- Dolly Parton
- William Blake
- Gloria Steinem
- Anne Brontë
- Edith Wharton
- Louise Brooks
- Betty White

- Virginia Woolf
- Maria Callas
- Morrissey
- Barbara Castle
- Ava Gardner
- Kim Cattrall
- Plato
- Nicolaus Copernicus
- Simone de Beauvoir
- Leonardo da Vinci
- Condoleezza Rice
- René Descartes
- Emily Dickinson
- Benjamin Disraeli
- Helen Mirren
- Sir Francis Drake
- T.S. Eliot
- Joyce Grenfell
- Florence Nightingale
- Queen Elizabeth I
- Chow Yun-fat
- Jean-Paul Sartre
- Dian Fossey
- Greta Garbo
- Celia Hammond
- Dorothy Parker
- Debbie Harry
- Steve Martin
- Iris Murdoch
- Isaac Newton
- Katharine Hepburn
- Bill Maher
- Joan of Arc
- Jesus Christ (shut up Dan Brown)

And don't start mumbling, 'What about Hitler...?' to the page. He wasn't able to have kids because of his well-known testicular limitations. Smart-arse.

In a 2008 Cambridge University report, which seems to suggest that support for gender equality is falling, it stated that in 1994, 51.8 per cent of British men and 50.7 per cent of women agreed with the proposition that 'a family does not suffer if a woman is in full-time employment'; by 2002, however, the figures had fallen to 42.2 per cent of men and 46.5 per cent of women.

Rachel Cooke, writing in *The Guardian* said, 'In all the maddeningly futile coverage of this survey I've read, no one has bothered to flip this thing on its head and point out that workplace discrimination and a child-obsessed society are entirely different things. So allow me. One hurts women, and society and, being historical, is unchosen. We must wipe it out. The other, alas, is entirely chosen, the result of a middle-class competitiveness that considers Mandarin classes just another notch on the Ikea yardstick of aspiration.'[3]

Parents appear to be involved in every aspect of the child's life now, and if they're not, if they put a foot wrong, woe betide the wrath that will meet them from other parents and teachers. And so play dates, all-inclusive birthday parties and stage-managed friendships ensue.

A day care centre in the United States recently stated, 'We don't discourage best friends like some other day cares and schools. We just encourage students to pick a non-traditional best friend, like a feather, a crystal that speaks to them, a zucchini, or a succulent.'[4]

If you read that and just think, 'Yes, that's sensible and thoughtful' I have no fear in pronouncing that you have lost your mind.

Then there's the story of Lenore Skenazy, author and founder of Free Range Kids and the co-founder of the Let Grow Foundation. She let her nine-year-old ride the subway alone because he asked to and was a good and intelligent child. After writing about it, she appeared on MSNBC, Fox, and NPR and was described as America's Worst Mom.

She says that in the course of every interview there was a moment when one of the hosts would lean over to her and ask, concerned, 'But Lenore, how would you feel if he never came home?'

Her view of this is that it wasn't a question. She thinks that to be a 'good parent' today you need to go to the worst-case scenario first, imagine that, and then act on that rather than reality.

It isn't completely the parents' fault that this has occurred. Despite violent crime in the States being at a fourteen-year low, a news diet of paedophiles, stabbings, and high school shootings is bound to have an effect.

Skenazy goes on to tell the story of a fifteen-year-old child in the United States who was out the front of his house chopping wood to build a fort for him and his friends. A neighbour called the police, who turned up, confiscated the axe, and admonished his parents.[5]

Skenazy points out that we've never lived in a more secure time, especially for children, and yet it feels 'like prison'. We are expected to know everything that is going on with our children, their texts, their friends, and their interests. Everything must be supervised.

Some of it can be traced back to the crime waves and hysteria around the safety of children in the 1970s and 1980s. In the United States, every morning families would see a missing child on the side of a milk carton (nobody explained that many were runaways or taken in a custody battle).

Skenazy asks in her book *Free-Range Kids: How to Raise Safe, Self-Reliant Children* (*Without Going Nuts with Worry*), if you wanted your child to be abducted, if you put your child outside, how long would you have to wait until they were? The answer, she says, is 750,000 years.[6]

The connection is often made that while we cosset children to this level, we ensure that their lives are devoid of anything resembling everyday life; the arguments and the skills required to confront and overcome such issues are managed by parents, and this has clearly led to the cultural changes seen on some college and university campuses.

The rise of the Social Justice Warrior, shutting down invited speakers who don't adhere to the agreed narrative, the requirement to have 'safe spaces' and trigger warnings for words that *may* offend one person and so on, these are merely the logical conclusion to this brand of parenting.

It appears that, to some extent, we are witnessing the death of education as feelings trump knowledge and any thirst to have your opinions challenged has been quenched by mummy and daddy telling you over and over again that everything you think and do is basically good and right.

Yeah, but saying no to children is bad! We should find other ways to stop your little boy smashing his sister's face in with his wooden bike. Oh Michael, try *riding* your bike.

Oh yes, sometimes the old adage is correct, blame the parents.

Gemma Collins, the 'star' of UK TV's *The Only Way Is Essex,* once explained she wanted to have a child to battle her 'feeling of unfulfilment' (sic).[7] And while it's easy to scoff at this hideous creature's self-absorbed musings, her sentiment will be shared by millions of prospective parents around the globe.

We're not all charmed by what your child just said, we don't think that having them constantly staring at us while we're on the bus is anything other than creepy and annoying, every conversation doesn't have to revolve around them; and here's a suggestion, try looking where you and your offspring are walking once in a while.

The Rod Hull Syndrome

*It's a funny thing about mothers and fathers. Even when their
own child is the most disgusting little blister you could ever
imagine, they still think that he or she is wonderful.*

Roald Dahl, Matilda

FOR THOSE THAT don't know, children's TV personality Rod
Hull's 'thing' was to place his arm inside the puppet of an emu, an
emu called 'Emu' that couldn't speak, and instead expressed itself
by snarling, or cowing when stroked. Invariably, the inevitable cre-
scendo to his act would see Emu attack children, chat show hosts,
and anyone else near to him by grabbing them round the neck and
the top of the head.

Rod had a false arm slung over the side of the bird to imply Emu
was a sentient being and Rod his inept owner, incapable of control-
ling this mute menace. It always looked overly painful as a viewer, and
once the realisation dawns on you and the suspension of disbelief
fades, you see that Rod was in fact grabbing people roughly with his
own hand.

For years people have been enacting a version of this 'turn' with
their dogs, as the mutt on too long a lead would jump up, ruin someone's skirt, slobber on their trousers, eat their picnic, while the owner
says something like, 'Oh, do stop it, Fido!' false laughing with an eye

roll, instead of thinking to shorten the lead. Maybe it's an accident. Maybe.

The expectation is you are meant to love their dog as much as the owner does. And supposedly, the stroking of the dog gives its owner the feeling they are being stroked too.

This seems to have now graduated to children, and all without the need for a false arm.

How many of us have been quietly enjoying a drink in a pub or a coffee shop only to realise that a small Omen child is staring intently at you? A half smile later and it's still there, while the mum and dad, either oblivious to it walking off or looking on like the proud parents they are, do nothing. One presumes that their pride stems from their child being able to be weird or annoying to complete strangers. Hooray! A real asset to society you've created. Thank you so very much. The addition of another thousand-yard-staring-potential-menace is just what we need.

Often the parent will say something like, 'Miles, do leave those people alone!' They're all jokey and resigned to being unable to control this seemingly unstoppable three-foot-high juggernaut of eerie.

These parents aren't watching their child; they're watching us. They're watching for our reaction rather than whether their kid picks up a fork and stabs it into its eye.

We know what they're expecting of us at this point; we're meant to stop our conversation, our meal or whatever it is, and smile at the little thing. Smile and perhaps mouth the word 'hello'. Or actually say hello. Invariably the little wretch will just continue to stare.

A few more 'hellos' will follow, and yet nothing. This miniature Easter Island statue just waits for something. We don't know what and we don't care. We just want it to go away.

Following this impasse we'll look over its head at the parent; we'll give them a fake smile and one of those eye rolls that says, 'Kids! Aren't they a wonder?!' We might even try one of those 'beatific' smiles. The one that says, 'Lovely child, please leave it staring at us for as long as you want, we absolutely love it!'

Of course, what very few of us do is what we really want. The simplest and most instinctive reaction. To ignore it, usually resulting in the child wandering off and the parents being a little put out but really, who cares?

Other options might include getting up, walking past the child to the parents' table, and just staring at them without saying a word. See how THAT goes down.

It might seem a little petty, but you have to understand, this is happening all the time to any of us who dare to go to pubs or restaurants child-free. Virtually every single time we get this creepy, intrusive approach.

It must be that child-free people are like a magnet to these children. Perhaps they don't like the fact that we are having a dialogue, or look like we're enjoying ourselves. Perhaps they are bored with mummy and daddy and want to stare at someone with some life behind their eyes! That's OK! It's not so much the act itself, as the drawing out of the affair.

There are more radical solutions available to us, of course. I take my lead from the way we've societally turned smokers into pariahs at pubs. Let's create family areas in the pubs! Imagine, roped-off areas out the back, covered in sick, where the tables are made of plastic rather than wood, soundproofed so we don't have to listen to you loudly slow-talking, or the baby crying. Or you could just go to McDonalds, which is where the kids want to be anyway.

And that's another thing; does anyone think these kids want to go to a pub? They're not renowned for their rides and pits of plastic balls. But perhaps that's just a matter of time. We'll inevitably infantilise getting smashed like we seem intent on doing to everything else.

You want it all, don't you? Your spoilt little brain thinks, 'I've had a child, but that doesn't mean I should modify my life. I still want pub, so baby, come to pub!' Kids should be, and probably are, bored out of their tiny minds at pubs. It's where grown-ups go to bitch about their friends' new kitchen or boyfriend / girlfriend, not a playground; that's why they're full of glass, fruit machines, and sharp edges.

If we can be a little melodramatic though, you're a virus. You're ruining pubs like you ruined football and the cinema, colonising it like the most boring invading army in history armed with iPhones and Kleenex.

And these little Emus come in many forms, like the unsettling stares from the one in the seat in front of us on a bus. We can see that you're busy. Your Facebook feed needs attention immediately, and while you're telling a 'friend' you literally never think of that you're thinking of him or her, your kid gets to be bored and peer uninterrupted at me over the seat.

It's hardly the worst thing in the world, true, but this kid will probably grow up to have no idea about boundaries, other people's personal space, or how rude it is to stare at people. He or she will think that it's perfectly OK to ignore your own blood by burying your stupid head in your stupid phone.

So, well done. It's going to grow up friendless and get the shit kicked out of it.

'Oh stop it, Mr Misery Guts', you say, 'it's just a little child!' Yes, yes but you see, if I was in a playground, a school, or even a park then sure, I'd expect this but, not at MY places. Keep your little Emus under control; I'm not Michael Parkinson.

Spatial Awareness

...You don't want one of those things.

Steve Martin

PICTURE THE SCENE.

An old lady is walking down the pavement on teetering legs riddled with arthritis. She's weakly pulling her shopping trolley behind her, ably attempting to navigate the people that bustle along during the daytime.

Ahead of her she sees a potential obstacle, a mother. She is heading straight towards her, pushing a baby-laden buggy with one hand, and with the other thumbing her phone scanning her Twitter or Instagram feed for the latest insightful opinion, cheap seats hilarity, or life-affirming / jealousy-inducing image.

To her side is another child on one of those wooden bikes that parents seem to think are more 'ethical' and 'real' than plastic or metal ones (which is an interesting view when they are invariably packed away into an entirely unnecessary 4 × 4 Chelsea tractor or fuck-off estate that guzzles petrol like an alcoholic uncle drinks lager at a wedding).

As the old woman approaches them she realises they won't all fit on the pavement. The mother, her pushchair and children representing a wide load, seems so distracted by her phone that she won't ask her child to be careful or indeed to change the course of her push-chair as it ploughs dead centre on the pavement, leaving no room for the old lady.

What can she do? She slows down; she tries to catch the woman's eye, but when she isn't looking at her phone, she appears to be staring straight ahead, with a determined look of contempt for anyone who dares get in her way.

Then, just as the old lady is about to be forced off the pavement and into the road, at the mercy of traffic, the mother notices; she tells her son to look where he's going and pulls him in. She slows her buggy down and swerves it to the side to allow the old lady enough room to pass. They exchange smiles, and the old lady pats the boy on the head.

The old lady thinks to herself, 'What a nice lady, a considerate mother, I'm sure her kids will grow up to be lovely too.'

The mother continues to teach her children to be considerate, and not to expect crowds to magically part in front of them as they walk down the street, not to expect doors to open, not to expect people to be just like them, nor expect job offers to arrive simply by applying for jobs, promotions not to just happen, money not to simply appear in your bank account, relationships to not just work, happiness to not just happen, and so on.

The boy grows up with a sense of perspective, of respect for his fellow man and woman, for animals and nature; he has a clear sense of purpose and great humility and consideration. He studies, works hard, meets interesting people; he cures cancer, ends famine, invents new and free public transport, and enables space travel and environmentally friendly and everlasting energy sources.

He finds a way to expand our understanding of the universe, and with his guidance, people are able to raise their mental frequencies and a new level of human consciousness is born leading to peace and compassion in every corner of every planet.

He is crowned the King of Earth and, while rejecting the title, he uses the power to bring people of all nations, creeds, faiths, and religions together to embrace harmony, knowledge, and the pursuit of happiness.

That story is all true.

Right up to the bit where the woman with the buggy notices the old lady. In the real version I witnessed, a woman with a pushchair careers down the centre of the pavement like the *Titanic* on its maiden voyage, unwilling to swerve or observe any obstacles (people) until it's too late. The difference of course is that the iceberg didn't leap out of the way into a road and narrowly avoid getting run over.

You see, children aren't to blame for this kind of behaviour; spatial awareness and 'other people' is something we pick up either by being knocked down, bashed into, or told by our parents. As with all these things, it's you, not them.

There is a sense of entitlement that some parents appear to have that simply by having sex and not taking precautions you have somehow reached the zenith of human achievement. The entitlement grows and manifests itself in many ways. Not least in the utter disregard for other people in the street, especially those without children. And society is feeding the monster.

How many times have I opened a door to allow a parent with a child, in a buggy or not, half expecting even a cursory glance of acknowledgement, but instead we see that same Queen of England stare, straight ahead, as if these things just open mystically for you once you have birthed your pride and joy? Perhaps we should bow as you pass us, tug at our flat cap, and mumble, 'God bless you, your Majesty.'

Then there are the little parent and child parking spaces. Usually near the disabled ones. 'That's because we're important and need to be cared for in a special way', you think. No, it's because Mr and Mrs Asda want the vast sums of money you intend to spend now you've managed to discharge a kid. Kerching.

And yes perhaps it is nostalgia, harking back (and one does like a hark) to a time of MK1 Ford Escorts and 'Mary, Mungo and Midge', but I remember when a buggy was the same width as an adult human. My, haven't they've grown! These things are like a 4 × 4. A 4 × 4 driving full pelt down a narrow country road, knocking cyclists and stray cattle into the hedgerow while the thing strapped in at the front brays a song of oblivious contempt to all around it.

Ooh, I've got to have the latest Bugaboo Bee with alloy wheels and iPad charger and coffee holder! It's almost the only thing in favour of people wearing a papoose; at least you're not a wide load. Just a wanker.

And surely you know this is happening, yes? You were a normal human being once; you know how annoying and inconsiderate it is.

So the top tip here is, open your eyes, or be warned, eventually someone's going to be coming the other way on the pavement, mouth-breathing into their iPhone, with as little regard for you as you have for them, and there'll be a pile-up.

And you know what, if I see that, I'll probably allow myself a little chuckle.

Join Us...

I've never regretted not having children. My mind-set in that regard has been constant. I objected to being born, and I refuse to impose life on someone else. Living, it's awful for me. I can't on one hand argue the futility of life and the pointlessness of existence and have a family. It doesn't sit comfortably.

Robert Smith, The Cure

'SO WHEN WILL you two be having kids?'

It's the question many child-free couples or individuals will have been asked at some point. It seems innocuous at first, sort of a social norm, and an acceptable query. And of course, something that often comes from people that have just had a baby.

But it's like asking that enquiring couple, why did you two *have* a child? And don't get me wrong, it's something I think from time to time when I look at an ill-matched and potentially doomed pairing, or maybe just idly recall the divorce statistics, but of course, I wouldn't think to ask for a moment.

These earnest questioners are like the members of a cult with their glazed and unblinking eyes, imitation smiles painted on to a shiny emotionless face. Join us...join us...

The usual response to this is an awkward 'Errr' and a shifting from buttock to buttock. A non-committal 'Dunno really' maybe or perhaps if you're feeling brave and it's true, 'We just don't want them', but somehow that'll be viewed as raining on the parade.'

'It'll be your turn next!' They'll say with delighted yet somewhat threatening faces as they clasp their newborn to their chest. Like there's some kind of queue for this roller coaster of sleep deprivation. Or maybe it's like *Logan's Run*. Why not try carousel? Turn? Then of course if you do utter anything that alludes to your uncertainty of having one, you get a sort of puzzled, 'Really? Oh…'

They might even follow it up with a bold, 'Why not?'

It's been said by many that once someone has a kid, they can lose many of the useful social norms they had prior to that. A lack of time knocks the niceties into the ditch of forgotten manners. It's hard to think of a more personal and potentially upsetting remark to make. For those who *are* happy to be child-free it's more baffling than anything. But for millions of people it's a delicate and troubling question.

There are a slew of wish fulfilment responses available to you when someone asks you, 'When will you be having kids?' Here are a few starters:

- *But I have to put up with so much inane conversation now, why add to it?*
- *I don't know, why didn't you adopt?*
- *When I stop thinking the human race should be on a path to extinction.*
- *Not sure, by the way, is yours meant to look like that?*

They won't hear you though. You must join the cult. You must!

However, there aren't many cults that spend so much time telling you how hard it is to be inside it. The Bhagwan in this cult seems tired, miserable, joyless, and devoid of the charisma he or she once had, and the incentives aren't free love, living outside societal norms, mindless worship, and primal screaming. Well, maybe the last two.

Social media is full of posts and videos of mums and dads parentsplaining to their friends how hard parenthood is. Everything from what gifts to buy them / their kids, why they can't spend time with you, and everything is underlined with the life-crushing hard work you have to endure as a parent.

I think I can speak for most child-free people out there when I say that when it's 'explained' to us how tiring and hard it is bringing up a child, we think, 'Well, yes, obviously.'

This parental pity party has even spawned books by well-meaning middle-class parents like Jennifer Senior, to warn mums and dads of the perils and pitfalls at play when you bring a new life onto the planet.

Senior claims in her book *All Joy and No Fun* that being a parent is one of the last permanent commitments remaining in society and that it isn't family life that has changed, but the choices and entertainment now available outside of that which have made parenthood appear more burdensome by comparison.

It's led to humblebragging on an epic scale that, as the Ross Douthat says, seems to be another way of shaming those that have 'opted out of the parental mission altogether'.[8]

If you want to be a good advert for the continued populating of our poorly planet, stop complaining about being tired, or about life being so hectic that it's not leaving you enough time to finish watching *Stranger Things* while posting a selfie next to some 'interesting' graffiti.

Another cultish behavioural trait, borne often it seems out of necessity, is the conjoining to other couples that have children. These 'convenient' and sometimes strained relationships are often formed at school or nursery gates, or some sort of antenatal class. All of a sudden, the standards and criteria you had for friendship go out of the window. Instead, dinner parties, barbeques and hopelessly stilted conversations become the norm and a little piece of you dies.

An exercise in personality gymnastics ensues where you retrofit your passions and opinions to those of the people who have also bred.

Stereotypically, the female in this set-up makes first contact with the other couple. One of the men will draw the short straw and be forced to make small talk with their counterpart. Their tools are male stereotypes like football, film, local gossip, town planning, before moving on to geo-politics. With hilarious consequences. Not really. Now you're trapped like Colonel Abrams. It's a social prison you've locked yourself into. You're the bitch and the daddy. The con and the screw.

Still, better that than hanging out with child-free people, right? Those cold, grey selfish people who wander the streets with their dead eyes and loveless, empty hearts.

Much better to hang out with Nicky and James. I love them, don't you? Nicky's so sweet, and she's *so* funny when she's drunk. When she sang the whole of Fleetwood Mac's *Rumours* that night I could have died. *So* funny. And James is great, *isn't* he? Loves his music, you two get along really well, *don't* you? I've heard you talk about football? Haven't I? He's really funny too. Very dry sense of humour.

And all you're thinking is, 'Nicky is damaged and James? I hate James.'

Yes, but James is probably thinking the same about you. Nicky too. And the reason is, this didn't happen organically. You decided – unlike the generations before you – that you need some sort of Parent Borg mothership to dock with.

And these things expand too. More couples get involved, it's like a snowball rolling down a hill, a snowball that slowly fattens as it reaches middle age, becoming bores who chime in with their pearls of wisdom about a world that they no longer know anything about because somewhere along the line they didn't have enough time to keep up with it, and yet clung on to the arrogant belief that they did.

'Oh yes, all the people who think X are like X. And all the people like us are right.' Tidy little platitudes you read via your Facebook feed of confirmation bias, or stolen from the five minutes of *Newsnight* you happened to catch. But because you're a parent, you're wise. People need to know what you think. It's important! I'm important!

Oh yeah, and guess what happens next? Divorce. That's right, the odds are pretty bad. Or good if you're a solicitor. In the United Kingdom it hovers between 40 and 50 per cent, as it does in the United States. In Europe it's even higher. And spare a thought for the Belgians and Spanish where it can get as high as 70 per cent. It's a lottery.

Then what? Who gets Nicky and James? Actually, that might be a blessing.

One doesn't want to be a moaning Minnie, and it isn't exclusive to parenthood of course; many friendships are created in a laboratory between couples, but this phenomenon is child-sponsored. You're friends, because at the age of four, your kids are friends. How long for? Yet you've taken the drastic step to make a friendship on this quicksand. You're insane.

So remember that when Nicky offers you the Kool-Aid. Don't gulp it all down at once. We accept you, one of us! Gobble gobble...

Your House Is a Mess

*'Looking after children can be a subtle way of giving up', said
Julia, smiling at Robert sternly. 'They become the whole ones,
the well ones, the postponement of happiness, the ones who
won't drink too much, give up, get divorced, become mentally
ill. The part of oneself that's fighting against decay and
depression is transferred to guarding them against decay and
depression. In the meantime one decays and gets depressed.'*

Edward St Aubyn, Mother's Milk

HOW LONG DID you spend choosing your home, and how much
did you spend on it? It was your pride and joy, your dream home, all
that money on a new kitchen, decorating the place, getting all the
right beddings and fixtures, those just oh so perfect details that
really 'make it your own' and are just 'so you'.

All those pristine white walls, country-style kitchen units, the
Pinterest boards that you showed to your friends and to your col-
leagues at work. Those back and forth emails and phone calls with
builders, going through the quotes until you decided on every room.

Then what did you do? You turned your house over to what is
essentially a mentally ill dwarf with destructively nihilistic tendencies
and no artistic merit. It transformed your house into a squat, a really
expensive mess that, because you're too exhausted to actually sit

back and admire it, you don't notice anymore, and if you did, there's little point in doing anything about it as the little whirling dervish will simply create an art installation of vandalism in the front room using sand or glue or peanut butter.

You may as well have bulldozed the house, filled the hole with plastic balls, thrown in a load of toys and covered it with a tarpaulin.

Now, before someone else gets in a strop about this and that, bemoaning those that live in a space-age, clinical house with sharp edges and easily accessible bleach, versus the loving chaos and 'real-ness' of their home, I concede, kids will be messy and that's OK (ain't I kind!). My brother's bedroom was filthy for instance. It always looked like the police had raided it (actually, they did once and it looked tidier. Little tip there.). That is not the point though; my mess was confined to my room. Rules are rules.

There's also something to be said for the rite of passage of being made to tidy your room and obey certain guidelines (just ask that Jordan Peterson fellow who's making a pretty penny from explaining the bleeding obvious to feckless, 4chan-dwelling MRA hobgoblins of hatred).

When you finally break off the shackles of childhood, get a job and move in to your own place, you embark on a voyage of discovery: I don't have to make my bed. I don't have to wash up. I can wear these pants again! Then you learn. You learn that you can choose to tidy up or not. You can live like Withnail, or you can actually behave like someone that people might find trustworthy, dependable, and responsible, and with a level of self-respect.

Today, parents spend four times as long with their kids than in any other generation, and have given over their house as their own personal playpen. Toys, god-awful drawings, crayon scrawls on the wall, miniature death trap cars or dolls and of course, uneaten sandwiches or crisps stuck down the side of the sofa.

It's not a sign of love and tolerance by the way; it just comes across like you've given up. Maybe you have. Or maybe you've accepted who really wears the (short) trousers.

It's not normal. Don't fall for that stuff. Just because all the other mums and dads say they have a messy house too and that they don't know how they'd manage without their Romanian cleaner. And before you get all argumentative, a working mother in twenty-first-century Britain spends about two to three hours a day more looking after her children than a stay-at-home mum would have done in the 1970s.

It probably stems from a multitude of reasons, some more serious than others.

Possibly the most alarming one is a thread throughout much of the problems with modern parenting. Children are being elevated to a level of miniature gods. They are the alpha and omega of our existence, and so *of course* the house is theirs.

Rory Stewart, a UK MP at the time, recently stated that children are now 'the opium of the masses' saying that we "accept too easily that the young should not be called upon to carry the burden sustaining communities because 'their lives are too busy'" and that there is a greater dismay at youth unemployment than there is at pensioner poverty, while all political debates hinge on the 'interests of the next generation'.[9]

He argues that while in the past we revered our ascendants, this is the first generation that, without God, conquest, adventure and honour, we find our greatest fulfilment in our descendants.

This cannot lead to anything good – a generation of children that grow into adulthood expecting everything to be tidied away, for everyone to tolerate their slovenly and selfish behaviour. We used to call this sort of mindless indulgence of children 'spoiling'. Now we call it modern parenting.

I'm not saying everything needs to be squared away all the time, but if your kids come to my house and touch any of my records, or start thumbing through my early editions of Alice in Wonderland, I will put them in the ground. Just so we're clear. K?

Then there are the other trappings. Hands up who's got one of those black-and-white portraits with their kids? Probably giant-sized and above the mantelpiece. Maybe it'll feature you all resting your stupid grinning faces on your hands. It goes with the wicker owls next to the TV, doesn't it, and the shabby chic chair in your farm-house kitchen you bought for £150 from that shop Retro Rascal or something. Yeah, nice to have all that rustic charm as you eat farmers' market gluten-free pork pies, and pretend to listen to your kid while actually playing Candy Crush or committing online adultery.

Where might it end? The unwavering acceptance of all their thoughts and desires will teach them nothing about life's realities, about how to function and learn as a human, and when they come up against each other in the real world of course, what then? A pair of individuals both convinced they are right, unable to accept criticism or instruction and yet desperately struggling to be understood.

Perhaps the universe will find some way of dealing with this. I picture student dwellings where every young adult is so messy that through some strange quirk of science the house miraculously tidies itself.

Or maybe automation will truly find its place in our future at that point, and instead of wasting its time helping us further human thought and our evolution, it'll simply pick up all the shit your chil-dren leave on their floors rather than cure cancer or FINALLY provide us with jet packs.

Maybe it'll just do an artificial intelligence shrug, build a rocket, and fuck off somewhere else.

They're Not Special

The self-esteem movement revolved around a single notion, the idea, the single idea, that every child is special.
Boy, they said it over and over and over, as if to convince themselves. Every child is special. And I kept saying fuck you. Every child is clearly not special. Did you ever look at one of them? But let's say it's true. Let's grant this. I'm in a generous mood. Let's grant this proposition. Let's say it's true as somehow every child is special. What about every adult? Isn't every adult special, too? And if not, if not then at what age do you go from being special to being not-so-special?
And if every adult is special then that means we're all special, and the whole idea loses all its fucking meaning.

George Carlin

IT'S BEMUSING HOW blind parents are to the concept of their child being special. Some even start these proclamations with 'I know everyone says this about their child but...' You know that bit at the beginning of the sentence doesn't help, don't you? You're just admitting the folly of your thinking as if it'll magically make everything OK.

Some kids *are* special in different ways. And some kids aren't. And what do we mean by special anyway?

Putting to one side the other use of special, there are genuinely special children, and we all know that. We probably know one or two. A friend of mine has a little girl who is extraordinarily intelligent, academically prolific in every subject from art to humanities to science, has a sophisticated sense of humour, is polite, kind and humble and she's not out of high school. That's special. Especially given that her dad is a complete moron.

But what makes the whole situation more special is that while the parents are clearly proud of her achievements, they wait to be asked. Which shouldn't be rare; that's how conversations work. You must remember: Someone asks you something, you answer, you ask a question, and you're away! You don't start yapping like a little dog advertising your progeny.

There are other kids who can be fun, easy-going, and occasionally funny; they have their trials and challenges, and guess what, that's normal, it's lovely and it's not special.

Rudolf Nureyev said, when asked why he didn't have children, 'They wouldn't be as good as I am, and then I wouldn't know what to do with the little imbeciles.' Brutal yes, but then, he knew he really was special.

If you recall the Roald Dahl tale of *Charlie and the Chocolate Factory*, there were children in that story who were meant to be the contrast to Charlie. They were brilliantly drawn representations of greed, selfishness, avarice, and other hideous character traits.

We now appear to be in a world where children are lauded for behaving like Veruca Salt or Violet Beauregarde. Again, we are confronted with children in advertising behaving in the most disagreeable and plainly counterfeit manner as if they were created in a laboratory.

Look back at the way children in the *7Up* documentary appeared and the contrast is clear. They're mostly humble yet honest and so brilliantly unaware of the camera. Now look at the children in programmes like *The Secret Life of 4 Year Olds* and the difference is not only stark, but also fairly depressing.

For the most part the children appear to be acting in a way that an adult might think one is meant to act. Lots of sideways, knowing looks, eye rolls, and comments that they've learnt to trot out because their parents have told them how funny it is, and it's become their party trick.

It's reminiscent of the phenomenon of cats on the internet, where our expectation of cats is for them to high-five their owner or to look good in a jumper they've been made to wear. And of course, all on camera! If people are capable of returning animals to shelters because they aren't photogenic enough or don't go with the décor of the house, they're capable of anything, so training your child to be a Macaulay Culkin prototype is a simple leap to make.

A 'conversation' broke out on Twitter recently around the current surge in young children 'being' transgender. As is usually the case, many people saw this as a great opportunity to make the discussion all about them and perhaps enhance their online id. That's the new normal now. But what was more fascinating was how so many parents chipped in explaining that being transgender made these children more 'special', that they were more mature, with one saying they were 'more evolved and kind', while another stating that these kids have 'come to teach us to love at the soul level, the way God loves us'.

You see, if you can wade through the theocratic woke-fuelled fuckery of these imbeciles, there is an inevitable conclusion; as the man says, if everyone's child is special, none of them end up being special. And parents are starting to realise this. Say what you like about humanity, but we're certainly adaptable. And competitive as hell.

If your reasons for having children were less than sound and you've turned this poor little thing into a medal for you to wear on your social media chest, then everything's a league table.

A scoreboard for the bored and terminally insecure.

Piano Prodigy	1	(Undiagnosed) Asperger's	4
Sixer at Cubs	1	Selfie with dad gets 50 likes	5
Nut Allergy	1	Trans	7

It seems for some parents, the fact that it's *your* child isn't enough. That you and your partner have managed to have a child and aim to bring it up to be happy, kind, intelligent and humane is great. But even that's not special. Special is the sort of thing that can change the world in some way.

So unless you give birth to a fully formed, adult female Nobel Prize-winning scientist vegan, who is mad keen on adopting kids and has a great sense of humour, shut up.

Who Are You?

Children aren't colouring books.
You don't get to fill them with your favourite colours.

Khaled Hosseini

THOSE DUMMIES THAT give the baby a moustache, those strapped to your chest baby carriers, and tiny Ramones T-shirts for kids. It's all the same.

This is you screaming I HAVE A CHILD, I HAVE A CHILD, AREN'T I SPECIAL! LOOK AT ME! I'M MORE INTERESTING NOW, AREN'T I? YOU THOUGHT I WAS DULL, BUT I WAS ABLE TO DO THIS AND SO I AM NOT NOW. I HAVE CULTURAL REFERENCES THAT I PLASTER ON MY CHILD LIKE IT'S A BILLBOARD. A BILLBOARD ADVERTISING MY YOUTH! TREAT ME WITH RESPECT! TREAT ME WITH RESPECT!!!!! AHHHH! MY BABY! LOOK AT THE BABY! LOOK AT ME!

The theory that some have children as a natural extension of their identity is not a new one, and with the rise of identity politics, a child is the perfect appendage. And as with all these things, there's nothing wrong with stretching the truth. So what if I don't really like AC/DC; just allow me drape the vestiges of yesterday's rebellion on my kid, will you?!

Think this is an exaggeration? Look at the world; look at the goods in the shops. I came across a Father's Day card that simply read, 'Cool

Dads Have Cool Kids.' They don't, for starters, and if they did, they wouldn't buy those cards. But aside from that, picture the hideous conceit on display here.

However, there's arguably so much pressure on parents these days – they're constantly told that parenting is the most difficult job in the world (it's absolutely not of course) – that it perhaps forces them to feel they need to live their life through their kids. And so they begin to lose sight of what they are. So your child becomes synonymous with your identity.

There's barely a parent I know who doesn't feel somehow legally bound to have a picture of their kids as the screensaver of their phone – something which has always looked to me a little like that scene in the 1970s Christopher Reeve Superman film where General Zod and his pals are imprisoned in a sheet of glass.

Replacing a picture of you with one of your child on Facebook is a perfect personification of this too. For starters, your child doesn't have a say in this. They may not want to be associated with your half-baked theories on Brexit / the homeless / religions; your latest 'gag' about Donald Trump; your endless empty, insincere yet carefully calculated opinions; or your tedious reminisces about Hong Kong Phooey or how much you fancied Zammo's girlfriend in *Grange Hill.*

Your off-colour remarks and edgy pub views have migrated to the garden shed of your life, and now, front-of-house are your children instead. It's easier than maintaining a personality I guess.

You can't, on the one hand, spill your vitriol about an *X-Factor* contestant and their ugliness and then go back to being this constant affirmation parent. It doesn't wash, sunshine. That contestant is someone's son or daughter too.

Currency in social media is important. How do I get more attention? I need affirmation. I need my belly rubbed. Oh, I know, another picture of my kid! And you're in this weird 'Like' club, aren't you? You 'Like' their child, they'll 'Like' yours. A *quid pro quo* of 'Likes' and some 'Oh, he's so cute!' and 'Has your eyes' and other hollow comments.

The 'Likes' and comments at first might be genuine, as you all welcome a new human to the world, but after that, one suspects they are going to be either politeness or pity, or most likely of all, an exercise in point scoring.

But it's OK, because you'll still make sure your kid is on-brand by captioning the pictures with your own inimitable sense of humour. It's all about you really, isn't it? Your kid is just a comedy prop for your Carrot Top turn. These poor little things are just a pair of funny spectacles for you to wear, an arrow through the head while you bounce around trying to catch our eye like a toddler looking for a 'well done'.

And they mean you don't have to offer anything genuinely interesting or amusing to say. Instead, we get treated to a picture of your little one sloppily drinking something with the caption, 'Looks like me after a few pints.' Oh yes, LOL, LOL LOL LOLlity LOL.

I saw an image on Facebook recently, and there are many, many, more, of a young mother holding her baby boy. She's Photoshopped stars around both their heads. Nothing unusual about it, you'd think. Except she's also Photoshopped both their faces so they appear unblemished and almost Manga-like. Her child is just one of millions of unwitting actors in a parent's play of mad insecurity and narcissism.

And on that, what about parents who turn every single conversation around to their children? It's real, and it smells of mental illness. You must have had these:

'What are you doing this weekend?'

'Well, it's Finn's piano lesson on Friday, so we'll be staying in, and then Saturday Audrey wants to go shopping, so I'll be taking her to...' Blah. Blah. Blah!

You can spend ages talking to these people and know nothing about them, how they feel, what they're interested in, what they'll be doing. Instead, you're treated to a rundown of their child's activities and preferences.

No one, not your closest friend or relative, has the same connection or empathy to your child as you do. Photos of children used to be something that grandparents would ask to see, but they've become a sandwich board you wear all day. Like one of those baby carriers. Those things you see dads wearing with the baby fixed to the front like that mutant in *Total Recall*. It's a child, not a coat of arms.

We live in a time when, despite endlessly discussing the demands of parenthood and unmatched levels of safety and health for kids, we've managed to arrange it so that parents spend more time with their children than at any point in recorded history.

That's fine. I mean, it's not, but it's up to the parents. What's not 'fine' is why the rest of us have to be subjected to this mania.

Ooh Look at Me

When I was 28-years-old and a girl said to me, 'Do you like children?' I'd go, 'Well, you know, not right now, but I think someday.' That was a complete lie. I never liked children. I never wanted children, and I was just saying that because I didn't want to lose the fish that was on the end of my hook.

Bill Maher

ONE DOESN'T WANT to criticise the women who wear 'Baby on Board' badges on the underground in London. Of course it shouldn't be necessary, but I've seen many a neck-bearded, stork-legged hipster fail to give up their seat on a train for a lady with eight months or so of infant inside her.

But I have NEVER understood the stickers on cars. As the comic Paul Foot said, 'This is not a ship, it is therefore not appropriate to talk about anyone "on board".'[10]

Apparently, it was originally developed to notify emergency services that arrive on the scene that there might be a child inside, but it doesn't seem to be used in that way now. Besides, that seems a little redundant anyway. Just look in the back, right? Rather than scouring the mangled chassis for a now crispy sticker.

I recently witnessed the epitome of the 'Ooh look at me' parent. I was on board a train, and a few seats down from me were a mum and dad with their small child. The man took it upon himself to narrate everything to his child. Everything. I counted one question from the kid regarding trains and then away dad went with his chronicle. Every scene we passed on the train, the inside of the train, the reasons for the existence of trains, other modes of transport, and so on.

That's OK. I'm not a monster! But this individual talked not only non-stop, but at a volume that was so deliberately increased and unnecessary, and coupled with his constant looking up and around into people's faces, including my own, to make sure we were all paying attention, it can only have been, at least in part, for the benefit of me and other passengers.

One wonders what impression he hoped we'd have of him. I posit he thought we'd think things like, 'Oh what a lovely dad' right up to 'What a knowledgeable and sexy dad he is!' Of course, all I thought was 'Shut up, you fool. Shut up, please God.'

He reminded me of that well-known 'fact' that sharks die if they stop swimming. He would simply expire if he stopped talking loudly to his son who, after about three minutes was not even replying and was no doubt thinking in a similar vein to me. *Please, Dad. Please shut up.* Alas, that poor child had at least sixteen more years of verbal assault ahead of him.

On another occasion I witnessed a man with a small child coming out of a pub, I opened the door for him, and as he walked out he said, 'Welcome to my life' and did one of those snuffly, snorty laughs at his own self-aware hilarity.

Be quiet. You wanted this! You chose it. You think there's something cool or endearing about you pretending to be the put-upon dad? There's not. Just say 'thank you' for holding the door, shut up and move on.

To revisit the pub scenario for a moment, you parents are ruining them too. It won't be long until adults who want a child-free evening have to go to that pub that you always walk past – the ones with the bright lights, blank stares, with moth-eaten and stained pool tables that do a roaring trade in Christmas lunches for familiarly expelled alcoholics and ne'er-do-wells.

Oh yes, these days the only thing missing in many pubs is a gigantic pen filled with plastic balls. You parents, you turn up, your treasured brood in tow, blocking up the bar with push chairs while your kids throw balls around and hit an elderly couple with them, while you once again give that shrug apology that is meant to say, 'Kids eh! What are you gonna do?!'

That shrug doesn't mean that to everyone else. Again, because we are not a planet that orbits your child, we just think, 'What an awful brat grown from the loins of this disgrace to humanity.' And don't be fooled, we dress it up as a faint smile and shuffling in our seat. There's hatred in that shuffle. To not coin a phrase, it is the shuffle of hatred.

There are of course many things you can do. Start by not thinking that because you want, it doesn't mean you should get. That's a good lesson for your kids by the way.

Then there are the clothes. In particular, those T-shirts mentioned previously. T-shirts on little boys that say things like, 'Trouble', or 'Lock Up Your Daughters' or 'Ladies Man'. No, they're not cool. It doesn't raise a smile with me. It makes me think, that child is basically your way of being a lad of the 1990s again. But it's ironic, right? Yeah, I've turned my kid into an ironic joke! Nice one.

How about a range of little T-shirts with a picture of an arrow pointing up and a slogan saying, 'I'm with the mouth-breathing imbecile staring into its phone. Pity me.'

You chose to have kids. You've made this monumental change in your life that you tell us turned you into a better person. It's the best thing you've ever done, isn't it? You can't imagine life without them, can you?

So how is it that you feel the need to continue to try and do all the things you did when you were child-free? You wander into pubs like a beheaded queen in a ghost story, cursed to revisit the places you once frequented. It's time for an exorcism.

You're So Boring

Needy and boring parents tend to have
needy and bored children

Amy Dickinson

I'D LIKE TO commit to record a genuine conversation I heard in a pub recently. I wasn't eavesdropping, I wasn't even on the same table as these people. They happened to be talking very loudly, and while I am tempted to recount the entire conversation on the basis that it would demonstrate the banality as well as the insanity of it better, I don't feel it fair to inflict this on you as well, dear reader.

Picture this: Mother with baby at pub garden table. Partner sat opposite. Their child was called Boden (pause for eye roll), and the parents were discussing their wills, very loudly, and moved on to how they should never fly together again. The reason for this was in case there was a crash, neither of them would be around to look after the baby.

Just let that sink in.

Aside from the eye-widening dullness and self-absorbed nature of the topic, it's just another, more morbid demonstration of how some parents can entirely surrender their lives to their children.

It starts with you kicking off the ear splitting 'Let It Go' sing-along with your three-year-old in Pret a Manger while patrons look on, wincing in disbelief at your behaviour. You've become a shit clown at an endless children's party. You'll be there when your kid is a teenager at a gig, singing into their face. You're not a parent so much as a cheerleader who manages fun and interests.

I know of a woman (there are plenty of male examples too, perhaps more) who was obsessed with the actor Anthony Hopkins. Completely. So much so, that no matter the conversation, she would be able to turn it in Anthony's direction. For example,

'We're going to the bakery to get some croissants, do you want one?'

'Anthony Hopkins' father was a baker.'

Also, I know of a mother who turns every question or situation into one about her child. For the sake of anonymity, let's call her child Treasured Being.

Ask her if she saw the new Meryl Streep film, and she'll answer it with something like, 'Oh, Treasured Being doesn't like serious films so no. We did see the new Star Wars film though as he likes that. He really likes that new character. The one with the spaceship? He said he can do all the moves on his video game. I'm rubbish at the video game, but he's ever so good.'

This person also put in her CV, in the bit that says, 'About you': 'Having a son about to start his GCSEs.'

It's tragic to hear someone talk as if all sense of his or her own identity and desires has been lost. Or at least have transferred a child's on to theirs. They appear to live vicariously through their offspring, enjoying things only if it 'works' for their kids, hating or avoiding things because of their kids.

I distinctly remember enjoying the fact that my parents hated the things I liked. And vice versa. I sometimes philosophised as a child, not grandly I'll grant you, that my mum and dad deliberately watched *Upstairs, Downstairs* to annoy me. Or ward me off. Hudson was the crucifix to my miniature Dracula.

Of course, the entertainment industry cottoned on to this many years ago. There are now children's animated films that grown adults now talk about like they've just watched *The Third Man*. Oh you go with the kids, but there's a lot for adults to appreciate, isn't there? They do some of those subtle jokes just for the grown-ups, don't they? So clever, isn't it?

No! Disney *et al.*, twigged this years ago and have been fleecing your stupid pockets ever since.

You're still edgy though, right? Still got a fingernail on the pulse. You watch *Jools' Annual Hootenanny* every year! Sometimes you even wish you were there, hobnobbing with Ade Edmondson, Lenny Henry, Eddi Reader, Paul Whitehouse, Rowland Rivron, Martin Freeman, and Jimmy Page. And you know what's real. You understand people. You've made friends with *The Big Issue* seller on the High Street for God's sake! Well, you say hello to him and buy a copy. But never read past the cover.

And you've got a good handle on politics, right? You watch *Question Time* on the BBC whenever you can, mainly to tweet about it with the hashtag to keep up the online persona you've built and ensure that girl with the blue hair likes your tweet. And you often agree with the trite and ill-informed views spouted by whichever fuckwit comic is wheeled in that week – because what politics needs more than anything right now is someone even more out of touch, egotistical and self-serving – and you tut and shake your head as a politician talks about cutting benefits, and the next night you laugh at some hapless poor people being followed by a film crew as they fumble to make sense of their wretched lives.

British singer Jessie Ware appeared on BBC's *The One Show* and, when asked what's the most rock-and-roll thing she's ever done, answered that it was that she was taking her eighteen-month old baby with her on tour. That entire sentence is possibly the least rock-and-roll thing ever written down.

Let's face it; having kids can make everything a little more boring. Late nights, films you *need* to discuss afterwards, they're lost on a bleary-eyed mum and dad who can't manage to utter a syllable of sense after 10:00 p.m.

Kids aren't necessarily boring, but family life that revolves around them can be. And that's OK. Take a look at sitcoms, for example. When kids are introduced, they clearly jump the shark. Gone is the tension, the drama and edge that made them funny. In comes a cosiness and banality that essentially destroys comedy. Only *Fools and Horses*, *Not Going Out*, *Parks and Recreation* all suffered at the tiny hands of infant introduction. While it's obviously a symptom of a series going on too long and running out of ideas, the introduction of children is the final nail in the coffin. Is it a reflection of real life? No one's saying that. But adults can be interesting enough without them, funny even.

Think of the greatest sitcoms there have ever been and imagine them with children: *Fawlty Towers*, *The Good Life*, *The Young Ones*, *Father Ted*, *Blackadder*, *Cheers*, *Steptoe and Son*, *The Larry Sanders Show*, *Frasier*, *Curb*, *Spaced*, *The IT Crowd*, *The Office*, *Seinfeld* . . . the list goes on.

If you watch *George and Mildred*, the classic 1970s UK sitcom featuring a warring working-class couple that are transplanted into a middle-class street, the only child is a complete brat. And it's funnier for it.

The entertainment industry has been undertaking the exact same tactic as many parents, furiously trying to convince us that children are cute. No exceptions. They're cute. Children are funny. They're adorable. They're smarter than you think. They're important, OK!

The reality is so, so different. Phone conversations become a futile attempt at communication, rather than asking your kids to be quiet; you are instead flung into that world, rather than being involved in a conversation.

Go to any of your friends' parties where people have either been encouraged to bring kids or have brought them because it didn't say don't bring them.

Parents inevitably peer over your shoulder to see if their child is trying to wear the cat or marry their sister to the garden rake by making her eat it; conversations aren't the order of the day. Instead, more often than not you get the communication version of a scratched record, jumping from section to section, invariably missing the good bits and finding the whole thing disappointing and a waste of time.

Watch as adults are asked not to smoke in the garden near the kids who have just run over to you. They're the ultimate killjoys and they're boring as hell unless they're yours. Imagine the disappointment of the child-free that turn up for a drink, chat, etc., to find the place overrun with knee-high wailing morons licking hummus directly from a bowl. Again, it's not that we hate your children, but there's a time and place.

Kids ruin adults' parties like adults ruin kids' parties.

It Doesn't Make
You Less Selfish

Man hands on misery to man. It deepens like a coastal shelf.
Get out as early as you can, and don't have any kids yourself.

Philip Larkin

SUPPOSEDLY WITH PARENTHOOD comes great perspective. The legend goes that once you have generously bestowed upon yourselves the gift of a child, you are suddenly forced to think about something else other than you.

This most selfish act will magically transform you from the awful self-regarding human you are into a Francis of Assisi character, unable to think of anything until you've thought of your child's well-being. Not only that, it's made you a less selfish person all round. You wander the streets picking up litter, delivering meals on wheels, housing refugees, and rescuing and homing stray animals. You'll find time to help other children less fortunate than yours, probably work in a charity shop and man a Samaritans line once a week.

You won't greedily guard the facile trappings of modern life; you won't broadcast your every waking moment on Facebook ostensibly using your child as currency, and you won't even own an iPhone because they're made by other children for a pittance of a salary in China. Poor things.

You'll reach a state of Zen-like calm because you will feel fulfilled, and rather than get into petty arguments on trains or in your car, you'll develop an approach that says, 'No my friend please, after you.'

As your friends we'll benefit greatly from this newfound selflessness. A birthday won't go by without a card from you; you'll constantly be in touch to ask how we are, and thankfully you'll make sure any interactions we do have won't be completely one-sided and revolve around your sprog.

The only reason you'll go to the gym is so you can prolong your life in order to spread love and tolerance throughout the world, and not to post images of your sweaty body, and carefully constructed gym outfit with something like 'I hate the gym LOL', or simply take black-and-white pictures of gym equipment paired with messages of horrible self-help garbage masking your pent-up frustration at a life wasted.

You'll genuinely help the environment because your child will have to live with the ramifications of our actions. Just popping plastic containers into the right bin won't do; you'll embrace green activism, stop using disposable nappies, and lobby politicians about factory farming rather than just buy organic eggs or go to the farmer's market and eat those awful gluten-free pasties.

Also, after your first child had this magical effect on you, you'll strive to make sure that you adopt number two or try fostering.

One can only think then that brutal battles for custody are simply a confusingly obscure act of altruism. That in fact, the interest of the child is at the heart of this conflict.

In October 2017, a story broke about a couple that had been going through IVF. They had a child in 2008 and then split up in 2010. However, the woman asked the clinic to implant an embryo that they had stored in the freezer, forging the signature of consent from the 'father' and had a baby daughter.

The father sued the clinic, demanding they pay for the upbringing and schooling of the child, calling her a loved but 'unwanted child'. The father lost the case, but the presiding judge was damning of the morals of the mother.[11]

It hasn't made people less selfish. It's a lie. One doesn't look at the world and think, 'Hey, we seem to be doing a great job looking after each other and the planet and all the animals. Hooray for us!'

Sure, for some people it can be 'the making of them', but too many become a horribly magnified grotesque of their former persona. They're just as selfish, probably more so; the difference is that you have expanded your selfish circle to include your child.

Then there's the surrogacy debate. It was recently brought to the UK public's attention as Olympian Tom Daley and his filmmaker husband Dustin Lance Black said, via social media, they were 'having a baby' accompanying the news with a scan. Amidst the predictably uniform glee from social media, some braver commentators suggested that firstly, two men can't 'have a baby'. Somewhere along the line a woman would have to be involved, and yet there was no mention of this.

The elephant in the room was of course, surrogacy. These two wealthy and successful young men had rented a woman's womb in order to have her carry their baby like the human allotment she is.

Of course, no sooner does someone raise the point of surrogacy and that it doesn't really mean two men are having a baby, than that someone is greeted by shrill and red-faced accusations of homophobia.

Once again, the argument is augmented by the belief that having a baby is a 'right', as are so many things these days like 'having a sex life' or 'being on the housing ladder'.

The happy couple themselves waded in implying that any reaction other than 'Oh, what wonderful news etc.' was homophobic and that UK surrogacy laws were bad and too strict.

A phone-in with LBC's Shelagh Fogarty had her shouted down as she tried in vain to address the surrogacy element of the story and ask why was there never any mention of a woman being involved in the media. The whitewashing of the woman involved was like some kind of Jonestown pact where we all had to believe in magic.

The truth of surrogacy is far from simple. In India, many women having babies for rich westerners are often pimped into surrogacy by their husbands.

Surrogacy, even more than IVF, smacks of the kind of narcissism that would make Hitler blush. Apparently, people with little or no understanding of genetics or the nature versus nurture debate hold his or her own DNA in very high regard.

Surrogacy is often seen as a 'progressive' cause, one that enables (particularly gay and lesbian) couples to 'have children'. It walks hand in hand with legalisation of 'sex work' and decriminalising drug use. However, aside from its clear avoidance of the adoption option, many women argue that it is a troubling and exploitative trend. Feminist icono-clast Germaine Greer warned that the very concept of motherhood was now being 'deconstructed' through the process of IVF and surrogacy.

Julie Bindel, a feminist and staunch advocate of gay and lesbian rights, wrote,[12] 'Fixated by vanity, imbued with overweening self-regard, they want to create a child in their own image, meeting a checklist of ideal characteristics. This kind of narcissism reached a grotesque logical conclusion in the case of the American lesbian cou-ple Sharon Duchesneau and Candy McCullough, both deaf since birth, who made the headlines in 2002 when they embarked on a search for a congenitally deaf sperm donor. Having been turned down by a number of sperm banks, they then approached a friend who had five generations of deafness in his family and was deaf himself. He agreed to their request, and a deaf child was brought into the world.'

It's also easy to see how this apparent dehumanising of the mother can be construed as misogyny. And from the very people who are potentially bringing new generations into the world. Bindel goes on to say, 'I was told that one gay couple had such loathing for the biological role of the mother that they even insisted that their (paid-for) baby should be born by caesarean section so it was not tainted by travelling down the vaginal canal.'

In 2014, a British husband and wife travelled to India with six eggs in refrigeration, and rather than do the usual and impregnate one surrogate, the husband said, 'I thought, get me two surrogates and implant three in each.' Four babies were then due, from two different women.[13]

When asked if they would meet their surrogates, the wife replied, 'She's doing a job for us, how often do you communicate with your builder or your gardener? She'll get paid...we don't need to see her... she's done a job for us.'

Another couple, when someone commented that one of their children was handsome, said, 'You get what you pay for.' Lovely, the commoditisation of children.

So, what about adoption? You're less selfish than us child-free, right? Adoption seems to be the ultimate act of human kindness. Yet I've heard people 'trying for a baby' respond to it as an option with 'oh they can be a nightmare' or often just let the question hang in the air uncomfortably till it goes away.

The impact on the kids not being adopted is of course colossal. Growing up in care is full of challenges. In the United Kingdom 20 per cent end up homeless in the first few years of leaving care, 50 per cent of prisoners under twenty-five are in care, and 22 per cent are unemployed.[14]

Of course, despite their claims of becoming less selfish, one can't lay all this at the feet of modern parents, but I'd be happy to admit that I am not contributing as much to society as someone who adopts or fosters. To claim that 'having a baby', by whatever means, makes you less selfish is patently false.

Between the years 1900 and 2000 the world's population grew from 1.5 billion to 6.1 billion. In 2017, it reached 7.6 billion. That seems pretty selfish to me.

Whitney Houston once said that children are our future, but at the risk of appearing smug (again), having a child comes just after transatlantic flights, eating meat, and driving a car in the league table of damage to the planet.

Disposable nappies take over five hundred years to degrade. So, in that way yes, children are the future. One that smells of excrement.

The Environmental Protection Agency estimated in the United States, that disposable nappies make up 3.5 million tons of waste each year being flung into landfill sites.[15] Add to that the 200 million trees that are chopped down to aid in the manufacturing of them and 3.4 billion gallons of fuel oil each year. The methane emitted from these nappies replaces oxygen and is dangerous to breathe.

Also, disposable nappies often contain dyes and dioxin, which is formed as a by-product of the chlorine bleaching process. Dioxin is a carcinogen, so it may cause cancer in humans and animals.

Not so cute now, are they.

Researchers from Lund University in Sweden recently found that having a child is the most environmentally destructive thing you can do. Obviously it found that we can all do more, but among its claims based on extensive peer reviews, it stated, 'A US family who chooses to have one fewer child would provide the same level of emissions reductions as 684 teenagers who choose to adopt comprehensive recycling for the rest of their lives.'[16]

Dolly Parton is one of the most prolifically successful and honoured music stars of all time; she is an immensely successful businesswoman, launched Dollywood, is funny and intelligent and remains child-free.

She's been married to her husband Carl for nearly fifty years, and together they helped raise many of Parton's younger siblings. But one of her most impressive achievements is her tireless philanthropy. Her Dollywood Foundation has helped in the area of child literacy as well as various animal welfare causes, the American Red Cross and HIV/AIDS-related charities.

She's endlessly asked about her 'lack' of children and has given a variety of responses ranging from 'I think I became more productive through not having children' to 'When I got married and wanted to have children I couldn't have any. But I don't miss it. I did for a while, but I realise that I am everybody's mother.'[17]

In a recent article, mother Lucy Mangan, compared the act of falling in love with your child the same as the beginning of a new relationship. 'You become an inward-looking selfish little unit of two for whom the rest of the world falls away.' She goes on to say that because it goes on for an inordinate length of time, it is not a mental state conducive to 'activism, altruism, or generosity of spirit'.[18]

If you were in any doubt that society was worshipping parents or at least parenthood, look no further than the financial benefits available to those clever mums and dads, none of which are available to those who remain child-free. The logic apparently being that they need more help from the state and should morally expect more in return, and child-free people need those children to pay the taxes and run the services that will look after them in their old age.

To any objectively minded person, this might feel financially and ethically wrong – the problem is it's another of those hot potatoes that politicians won't touch with a barge pole. As a voting block, families are high value to political parties and therefore sacrosanct because they tend to respond across party lines to any policy that affects their family alone rather than wider society.

With this kind of state-sponsored favouritism, one could forgive some parents for walking around as if they are the chosen ones. Almost. Believing they have created a miracle and are therefore entitled to adulation. As Bill Hicks put it, 'It's no more a miracle than eating food and a turd coming out of your ass. It's a chemical reaction, that's all it fucking is…it's not a miracle if every nine months any yin yang in the world can drop a litter of mewling cabbages on our planet.'

In a recent poll commissioned by Mumsnet, 18 per cent of parents admitted to buying or renting a house in the catchment area of a preferred school.[19] That's not helping your community, or being a good citizen. That's you, thinking of your child above anything else, including people that might have grown up there or are being moved out of the area by housing associations so they can sell flats to people like you. Work that into a chant at your next Sunday afternoon demo.

How is it that this parent worship has increased at the same time as the seeming epidemic of using au pairs and nannies? That's a strange one; surely, rule one of having a child is being around. And that's not to say it's a bad idea having an au pair or a nanny (it worked very well for the von Trapps after all); simply dispense with the feeling that you're not as selfish as the next man or woman.

Child-free people appear to find lots of worthwhile things to fill their time, stay happier than their counterparts with children, have better holidays and appear to give up more of their wealth to help society at large.

Russell James, an expert on philanthropy at Texas Tech University states that people without children are far more likely to bequeath money to charity, and in 2014, 48 per cent of married child-free couples had committed in wills to give something to charity.[20]

Yet this warm feeling of being better persists. In the 2016 leadership contest for the Conservative Party, candidate Andrea Leadsom, a mother of three, said the following about rival Theresa May who has no children: 'I am sure Theresa will be really sad she doesn't have children, so I don't want this to be "Andrea has children, Theresa hasn't" because I think that would be really horrible.'

'But genuinely I feel that being a mum means you have a very real stake in the future of our country, a tangible stake', she said.

'She possibly has nieces, nephews, lots of people, but I have children who are going to have children who will directly be a part of what happens next. It means you don't want a downturn but never mind 10 years hence it will all be fine, my children will be starting their lives in that next 10 years so I have a real stake in the next year, the next two.'[21]

She was rightly vilified for the comments, but it betrayed an unspoken, or perhaps spoken amongst parents, smugness and astonishing self-regard and magical position of privilege.

It crosses party lines, too. Labour MP Owen Smith odiously proclaimed that his 'normality' came from his 'wife and two kids'. Well, he's probably not normal for a start, and don't loads of MPs have husbands, wives and children? So, are the child-free ones abnormal, Owen?[22]

This didn't shock many of us as we've heard similar platitudes for years. 'Since having a child I've taken much more interest in the future...', and 'I've become far more ecologically aware since we had a child.'

As Cameron Diaz said, 'I think women are afraid to say they don't want children because they're going to get shunned. But I think that's changing now. I have more girlfriends who don't have kids than those that do. And, honestly? We don't need any more kids. We have plenty of people on this planet.'[23]

Of course, for some parents, parenthood has had a positive impact on their outlook; it has given them the jolt they apparently needed to wake up to what life can be like and instigate a positive change in their behaviour. Perhaps something was already there though, and that jolt could have been provided by another earth-shaking event such as losing a job, a health scare, bereavement or incarceration.

For others though, it appears to have been a magnifying glass to their appalling character traits and weaknesses, and there is no doubt that social media has done nothing to discourage or at least highlight this bad behaviour.

This book could be filled with pages and pages of quoted posts, tweets, and captions from parents on social media effectively using their child as a prop. But where is the fun in that? Many of us already glaze over at countless pictures of other people's kids with mum or dad somehow demonstrating how selfless they've become by promoting their brand of domestic happiness like some sort of Ikea Joseph Goebbels.

It's clear that for some parents their perspective has changed. It's grown much, much worse. If anything, people seem more selfish than ever, as they grip on to any identity that will further their sad little online trademark. In the words of Spinal Tap's David St. Hubbins, it's too much fucking perspective.

You're a Big Child Too

I do not want children. When I see children, I feel nothing. I have no maternal instinct. I am barren. I ovulate sand...I look at children and feel no pull toward them, no desire whatsoever. Actually, my fiancé and I have seen some very interesting personal ads of 50-year-olds that like to wear diapers. So we're thinking of adopting one of these guys. A baby by choice.

Margaret Cho

A RECENT STUDY claimed that overuse of mobile phones by parents is disrupting family life. Over a third of the eleven- to eighteen-year olds polled, said they'd asked their parents to stop checking their devices, and 14 per cent said their parents were online at mealtimes (though amusingly, 95 per cent of parents polled denied it).[24]

Not only does this fly in the face of the traditional perception that it's children who require discipline from the parents, but it also demonstrates a lack of awareness in the parents.

Remarkably, or perhaps not, 82 per cent of the children felt that mealtimes should be device free and nearly a quarter said the use of mobiles stopped their family enjoying each other's company. Sadly, only 10 per cent of parents felt their mobile use was a concern for their children. Many of these kids felt ignored and upset by this behaviour.

Take a trip down any social media timeline and it's almost indecipherably hard to differentiate the forty-somethings from the eighteen-year-olds. Perhaps spelling, perhaps a few more mentions of pop culture from the 1970s, and horribly, slightly more entitlement. Yet these alleged grown-ups are using emojis like it's going out of fashion and bleating on about their latest cause that they read about this morning and have thrown themselves into in the last five minutes with no research or actual commitment or understanding. Hooray!

It's enough to make you develop a permanent cringe as people in their forties talk about their love of unicorns, say babyish things like 'these bad boys', 'sorry not sorry' or 'because reasons', obsess like a teenager about comic book films and feel it's good to carry on that baby boomer mantra of unlocking your inner bloody child.

What happens once you've unlocked your inner child and decided to have one yourself? It can't be good, can it? Isn't our existence meant to involve some kind of learning, some kind of understanding of other people and nature that leads to an enlightenment of sorts? A humility that inspires someone to realise there is always something new to know, might be lost.

But no, let's waddle about in flip-flops like a petulant toddler, let's use love hearts and smileys all day to other adults, let's say things like man-flu and infantilise an entire sex – what harm could come of that?

It's demonstrated in that most ugly and sinister of activities when a parent becomes the 'best friend' of their child. This curious and growing phenomenon we hear from children and see from adults begs the question, what about their real best friends? And doesn't it blur boundaries? It might come from a 'good place' as parents try to compensate for the utter lack of interest their parents might have shown in them, but two wrongs don't make a right, and this one has the whiff of unhealthy co-dependency.

Whether it's posting something about ruddy well wanting to punch a Nazi while you live an idyllic, gentrified and leafy existence of (probably well-earned) privilege and detachment from the real world, or getting off the train in the suburbs and jumping on a child's scooter (A CHILD'S SCOOTER!) to travel the two-minute walk to your front door, you're as much a product of the infantilisation of society as anyone born in the 1970s or 1980s.

'Love my new bunnyrabbit backpack' posts the forty-year-old marketing executive on Instagram as he sets off on a five-mile bike ride with his friends. Garbed in Lycra and those unbelievably dorky helmets and expensively naff and unnecessary goggles, they stop off every now and then to fill their stupid little ergonomic water bottles at an artisan coffee shop and have some 'bants'. Then they'll clumsily attempt to dissect current events or the 'footy' they started watching in the 1990s since it became something they could talk about without having to mix with the dirty unwashed Neanderthals from the terraces.

As I reluctantly swerve my car around these hopeless two-wheeled herds, it often occurs to me that they have transformed themselves into giant sperms, racing the other plastic tadpoles around the country lanes till they get home to their egg-shaped wives.

From psychologists to sociologists to you and I, we witness the endless stream of comic-book and science-fiction films at the cinema, as slowly our sex-obsessed yet sexless society falls further into parody.

Simon Pegg, actor, writer and star of *Hot Fuzz*, *Star Trek*, and the cult UK sitcom *Spaced* said, 'In the 18 years since we wrote *Spaced*, this extended adolescence has been cannily co-opted by market forces, who have identified this relatively new demographic as an incredibly lucrative wellspring of consumerist potential. Suddenly, here was an entire generation crying out for an evolved version of the things they were consuming as children. This demographic is now well and truly serviced in all facets of entertainment and the first and second childhoods have merged into a mainstream phenomenon... We are made passionate about the things that occupied us as children as a means of drawing our attentions away from the things we really should be invested in, inequality, corruption, economic injustice etc.'[25]

And if you're lazily thinking it's not about you, just look back to the last time you used the word 'noms' to describe food, or maybe 'yummy' to describe a person, a piece of clothing (or food again). Perhaps you counted the length of time to an event in 'sleeps'? And you've certainly used emojis, haven't you?

And while we're on emojis, the effect on children using them is now being questioned. In a study published in the Oxford University Press, teachers described the 'word gap', with kids being held back due to a lack of vocabulary. It cited two major causes: never reading for pleasure, and too little in the way of adult conversation.

As Laura Freeman said in *The Spectator*, when kids say 'sad', they could now mean a plethora of negative emotions from mildly frustrated to utterly ashamed or neglected.[26]

It's common now to see adults with hats that have animal ears or backpacks branded with a children's cartoon.

Not only that, but you've posted this all over social media because you're proud of it. You actually *want* this to be your brand. Yes, an adult human who is talking like a toddler is able to create a life, go to prison and, most alarmingly, vote. 'Noms'? 'Want'? 'Need'? What they need is a smack round the head. Want?

It's as if their only way of expressing their *joie de vivre* is via a yellow face with its tongue sticking out. And I don't buy it. I'm not sure anyone does really. I think anyone determined to convince everyone else that they're happy and fun is quite probably neither of those things.

And their baby talk goes nicely with their alarm clock outrage at today's latest issue. They switch from putting Snapchat filters on their faces to abusing politicians or spewing their fresher's week, student union opinions and solutions on everything from what to do in (insert Middle East region here) to gun crime. Nom those yummy opinions.

We see it with every celebrity death as the cascade of dishonest sputum sprays onto our screens, 'RIP so and so, that's ruined my day! I really liked / fancied him / her (sad face emoji).'

Then there are the irritating men (yes, it is literally always men) who decide to ruin my Sunday morning (yes, Sunday morning) by flying a drone twenty feet above the ground that some complete bastard bought them at Menkind because they know what a pointless cretin they are.

What an apt name that is too: drone. These massive children are flying miniature helicopters above their garden to film – guess what – their garden. They should of course be redirected somewhere more useful. I have a list of more productive / appropriate alternatives: it starts with go away and ends with a one-way train ticket to Beachy Head.

Some can't resist bunging their sprog into the mix of any 'opinion' posts for added 'compassion' points. Kids are a handy tool for the avid armchair moralist. 'How can I look my child in the eye and say I did nothing?' when referring to them tweeting about an issue raised in parliament. With all this cognitive dissonance, it's horrifying to think what the child's reaction will be if they actually find out they're mummy and daddy's currency.

Parenthood doesn't make you grow up; it just enables us to see what would happen when a giant child has to look after a normal-sized child. And it's not pretty.

This Won't End Well

Children begin by loving their parents; as they grow older they judge them; sometimes they forgive them.

Oscar Wilde

OF COURSE, IF years of helicopter parenting and child worship leads to the world being gifted a generation of kind, selfless and mature individuals who contribute meaningfully to the world, then that'll be just dandy.

I'll happily join the queue of people ready to apologise. I'll have a copy of this book in one hand ready to burn as an offering at the feet of hideous parents, and in the other hand I'll have a map to the nearest multi-storey car park from which to leap off.

And while one hopes that the eventual backlash will come from these very children, the signs aren't good.

Alarming trend number one is obesity. The scourge of Western living is hitting millennials hard. According to Cancer Research, in the United Kingdom, around 70 per cent of people born between the 1980s and 1990s are on course to be obese before they hit middle age.[27]

Despite the plethora of healthy and low-calorie food options available to them, a gym in every high street, endless campaigns and the wagging finger of an increasingly 'nanny state', we appear to have a generation of budding fatties lumbering along the pavement.

In 2018, when Cancer Research UK, launched a campaign to raise awareness of the causes of cancer, one advert featured a cigarette packet full of chips, and the accompanying line, 'Guess what is the biggest preventable cause of cancer after smoking.'[28] The answer was of course obesity, and the outcry was dreadfully predictable. Accusations of fat shaming were levelled at the charity from a noisy (and one suspects short of breath) minority, despite the intention of the ad to counter the fact that barely 15 per cent of people were aware that obesity could lead to cancer.

If it hasn't happened already, expect to see more money invested to introduce reinforced suspension and super wide seats on busses and other public transport to cater for these excessively cosseted ravenous porkers. Why should fatty suffer? It's a condition, a disease even. Why not?

Despite everyone striving to be 'present' at the moment or to 'reconnect', whatever the holy bollocks that means, over a quarter of children in the United Kingdom between two and ten are overweight or obese, making it very likely they'll be obese adults. It is harder in some ways; there's sugar, salt and God knows what in so many things now. But children are having their teeth removed by dentists at very young ages because of the amount of sweets and sugar they eat. So yes, fat-shaming kids isn't a good thing; shaming the inept parents that (literally) feed this scandalous issue is maybe a tactic we should get behind. But only if that's OK with you piggy?

In the old days it was a running joke that someone on the plump side would claim to have a glandular problem or even better, be 'big boned'. We live in a world now though where it's all about metabolism and something called 'fatness', and while the clampdown on bullying in schools seems a good thing, perhaps this acceptance of someone who won't stop stuffing huge oozing Subways into their mouth as just another victim, isn't the best alternative.

One individual on Twitter said, 'I have to pass (the Cancer Research advert) three times on my journey to and from work and one of them is a house-sized billboard. I'm stopping ANY support of (Cancer Research UK) until they quit shaming me.'[29]

It's part of the recent tendency for people to immediately respond in an emotionally and bewilderingly self-centred way, rather than accept that they might be in the wrong or have something to learn.

These whingeing covetous lard-asses are surely the result of the same thinking that gave us non-competitive sports days, where children don't so much compete as unwittingly become part of some hideous social experiment. Inflicted on them by people, one suspects, who endured schooldays looking on jealously at the football and netball team players – only to find a way of getting their own back.

In a recent survey, 86 per cent of parents, whose children are at schools where sports days are non-competitive, disapproved.[30] So it doesn't work for the parents. Brilliant. As sports psychologist Amanda Hills puts it, 'This business of saying that sports days need to be politically correct, with no element of competition, to me that's absolute nonsense. It doesn't teach children anything useful, because life is competitive, and they have to learn to lose as well as win.'

Much better it seems that the competitive human spirit is instead inserted into social media, where kids can scroll through a compendium of unattainable imagery curated carefully by their friends and 'influencers'.

And how does this relate to parenting? It's not just tempting, it's patently obvious that helicopter parenting, and the obsession with children in general, has led to many young people feeling that, quite understandably, the world doesn't just revolve around them, but it should also know exactly how they feel all the time, and cater for them in every way.

Parents face enormous expectations to be God-like or perhaps simply enjoy this 'KGB for Kids' role. Pumped daily with paranoia-inducing advice and news stories, it's not hard to see why every parent doesn't fret endlessly at the danger their child is in every minute of the day.

Despite our privileged existence parents are micromanagers. There was the story from a parent who said she went to a playground with her child where the ratio was two adults to every child, and she had to ask one of the fathers to get off a piece of playground equipment so her son could use it.

It's not all gloom and doom though. Laura Skenazy's Let It Grow Foundation, in an attempt to combat this agenda, carried out exercises where parents are, for example, encouraged to let their children go out and get milk. She says that almost all the parents involved are 'ecstatic' at the end of the exercise and literally can't remember why they stopped them doing this in the first place. Her revelation, she says, is that the reason they are so happy is the realisation that when they die, their kids will be OK. A natural and undeniably profound concern.

Helicopter parenting has been around for decades now, but it has never been more prevalent. The emergence of 24/7 media, mobile phones, social networks, TV drama that appears to be obsessed with crime and murder, a litigation-hungry society and an expert culture where parents are bombarded with articles like '10 Ways To Ensure Your Child Doesn't Choke On Her Quinoa' have all contributed to making some parents slightly insane.

That's not to say that children should experience all the horrors of the world. I remember during the 1980s consuming a diet of *Threads*, *The Day After*, 'Two Tribes' by Frankie Goes to Hollywood, and most disturbing, Raymond Briggs' *When the Wind Blows*. It gave me nightmares for a few months and a healthy cynicism of the world and adults, and a view that ultimately, it was probable that humanity would destroy itself and everything else, so what's the point in anything.

Obviously that was just a phase.

There are of course many examples of horrifying overparenting and something we can all shudder at, and the parents can laugh at them thinking out loud, 'God, what a nutter', while inwardly perhaps thinking it's reasonable behaviour.

It can start small, the judging of another bleary-eyed parent at the primary school gates in the morning who happens to be chugging an energy drink, right up to the pages and pages of stories about

parents who turn up at lectures, schools and so on, inspect the sylla-
bus, even making wake-up calls every day to their kids who no longer
live at home.

Ask a teacher how they find parents these days, and they will usually take a sharp breath in as this fearful look comes over them. It
doesn't stop at school; employers have conducted interviews with
the applicant's mum present. They will apply for their child and even
try and negotiate the salary and benefits.

We used to call this 'meddling', and it was embarrassing to have
your parent involved in your life that much. But it's the natural pro-
gression for a parent who has fetishized parenthood and spoilt their
child.

In a recent article,[31] Kerry Porter grumbled that Britain might
have become an anti-child society. Her argument stemmed from
an experience in a café in Paris where she was eating with her kids.
According to Kerry, a British woman 'shot death stares' at her and her
family and then exclaimed to the man opposite her that the restau-
rant had too many children in it. If we ignore that this probably didn't
happen, Kerry then goes on to bleat about other establishments who
have rules around admitting under-twelves because they break too
much crockery and the battle for parents with 'adult travellers who
feel entitled to peace and quiet at 30,000 feet.'

She appears to be one of many parents who feel that, not sat-
isfied with a society that has bent over backwards for decades to
allow you to colonise every adult dominion with your progeny, and to
saturate culture with children and parenting till the rest of us simply
give in and draw on a stupid smile and let you fuck everything up,
you must also deny others the right to find your horrendous brood
undesirable.

Tell you what: let's see how it works the other way. I'll drink a
two-litre bottle of Diamond White, thrash and whirl myself into the
soft play area at the local playground and start demanding that the
children all sit down and talk about soft furnishings, mental health,
and Donald Trump's latest tweet.

There are stories of children of four, five, and six years old walking through the gates of their school wearing nappies under their clothes because they're still defecating themselves. Some teachers now work in classrooms with changing areas and are sometimes expected to change the children if they've soiled themselves.

Trawl any number of message boards and you'll find parents and teachers concerned about even raising the subject of certain kids (and not those with special needs) being too old to be wearing nappies, and they are berated by other parents telling them that they are being unreasonable and should 'keep their noses out'.

Most claim their children still wear nappies at four or five due to claptrap like, 'he / she wasn't emotionally ready to not wear nappies'. Now I'm no psychologist, but I would venture it's the parents who aren't emotionally ready.

You love all the trappings that result in the tedium of your Facebook and Instagram feed, or your stupid blog posts and penchant for moral posturing, but when it comes to telling your child to shit in a toilet, you're just not up to it. Emotionally.

Recently, the NASUWT teachers' union claimed that children as young as four are suffering from panic attacks, anxiety, eating disorders and depression,[32] while the Department for Education says that one in three teen girls suffers from anxiety or depression, an increase of 10 per cent in the past decade. Much of the blame has been placed at the feet of mothers. Mothers who let them watch too much telly, mothers who are too busy working, mothers who are 'too hung up on looks'.

The pressure is intense, as academics and self-help childcare experts pile more and more risks and fear onto the quivering shoulders of parents.

The question's been raised in this book and in many others before: Might raising children to expect a world full of mummies result in us having a whole generation of indoor cats? A population of humans so incapable of dealing with reality, that they can only live a life of misery? It's something that is staggering when you think we are living in a society that also seems so utterly obsessed with potential and children, that we are missing this particular elephant in the room. An elephant wearing a full nappy at that.

The millennial generation were predicted by many to be the most open-minded and tolerant; however, as Dr April Kelly-Woessner says, if you define tolerance by how you treat people you disagree with, they may well be the most intolerant.[33]

She says that tolerance is not a universal value, and that there is a 'tolerance paradox' where it is claimed that you should be intolerant of the intolerant. Therein lies the problem that there is no agreed arbiter of what is or isn't hateful or wrong and so we see intolerance on the rise.

So if you've grown up with parents idolising your every move, never saying no, and managing your life for you, we have what some Americans call a potential clusterfuck.

Not so much 'I disapprove of what you say, but I will defend to the death your right to say it' as 'I disapprove of what you say and I am going to call the police.'

The child that has his or her life treated like a pantomime for mummy and daddy and all of mummy and daddy's friends, who are also mummies and daddies, as they view the footage on Facebook in a hellishly never-ending zoetrope of gawping, belligerent brats careering around art galleries or supermarkets, will surely end up being the most awful human being imaginable and ruin the planet.

The odds are stacked in favour of the poor thing growing up to expect applause at every nose pick, every feeble joke or facial expression as they scrunch their brow when every relationship ends in a rejection they are incapable of fathoming.

And as you get older, you'll wonder why your little prince / princess is now a fifty-year-old narcissist who lives in squalor in *your* basement waiting for you to die. But boy, won't they love you? Actually, that's extremely unlikely. As they contemplate their life while Call of Duty loads, they'll blame you for everything because (a) it probably is your fault, and (b) they've had a lifetime of lessons in it not being their fault.

An acquaintance told me recently that her 'little brother' of twenty-two, on being left alone at her flat while she went to work, proceeded to make an almighty mess of her place. He ordered pizza on her credit card and defecated in the bath because, as he put it, Lad Bible suggested it would be funny to do.

This fully-grown adult male still gets an allowance from his parents, all the attention and infantilisation mummy can provide in person and via social media, and has a career plan to 'sell shares and make millions'. Once again, ladies and gentlemen, this man is twenty-two and one day might be advising you on a mortgage.

This David Brent School of parenting, where everyone's meant to be best mates with their kids rather than a useful authority figure, has surely helped usher in perhaps the worst period of comedy in history since the music hall.

Ten-part series are commissioned of some of the worst entertainment imaginable as gigantic wet children go on 'trips' with their mum or dad and we get to see how crazy a time they have in Vegas, the Deep South or the Norfolk Broads. These insipid and cosy programmes are an affront to anyone with any taste, but aren't they just another example of the obsession with the relationship of parent and child?

As you watch parents shuttling their children around in their 4 × 4s, walking in through a door you just opened with no acknowledgement, furiously posting their every move, it's easy to see why some see child worship as the new religion.

Because we've given up on God and church, we tried political ideology and it mostly didn't take, and science seems to just take care of itself and besides, it is a bit depressing, so parents expect children to fulfil them completely. There's nothing else.

There are altars of enormous framed photographs and strewn toys, the relics of baby clothes, rituals of school runs and clubs; there are bibles on child rearing, clergymen giving advice that contradicts your better judgement, different sects recommending different ways of worship, vestments and robes of papooses and car seats; there's a transfixed congregation at every barbecue and of course, a tucked away feeling that this may all be a waste of time and is papering over the cracks of an existential crisis.

The average parent will post a thousand images of their first child by the time they are five years old. It's not the kids who have changed, it's the parents and that's not love; that's the behaviour of a stalker.

I've seen memes created by parents featuring their kids' faces and accompanying 'jokey' messages like, 'All I want is two front teeth!' Another one I've seen has a photo of a parent's six-year-old daughter sleeping, and the line, 'When I wake up I will be 7.'

Congratulations, you've made your child a meme.

Apparently, we are biologically hardwired to think our children are the best to ensure we protect them. The difference is now we can advertise it. Endlessly.

It puts the child-free in the wilderness. Atheists in the midst of a fundamentalist cult, unable to be heard above the rabid fawning and written off as somehow missing out on the great truth.

But then the best functioning in society usually go unnoticed.

We know all these allergies and disorders are probably nonsense by the way. Despite us living in the most advanced era in human history with a population able to order organic bell peppers from your phone for your pet African teacup pig while Skyping silently to a meditation retreat in Mumbai, and retweeting a crowdfund page of your friends' twenty-two-year-old daughter so she can go travelling across Patagonia on her gap year, we are apparently at the epicentre of a mental health crisis in children and chronic obesity at levels never seen before.

Amidst the overabundance of celebrities celebrated for publicly airing emotional problems, from the cast of *TOWIE* to Prince William, and the rewriting of the way education is delivered in schools (including the decision to drop the word 'education' from the newly named 'Department for Children, Schools and Families' in 2007) there are concerns adults have left children increasingly 'vulnerable' and unable to cope with normal pressures.

In her book *Childhood, Well-Being and a Therapeutic Ethos*, Professor Kathryn Ecclestone of Birmingham University says that culture is 'saturated' with the language and mind-set of therapy.[34]

While carefully distinguishing those with genuine and major behavioural and emotional difficulties, she says that insecurity has been turned into 'a new genre, with a plethora of lifestyle experts, from cosmetic and fashion pundits to family therapists, focussing on the emotional vulnerability caused by life events, being middle-aged, lazy, having poor diet or lacking good dress sense.'

She goes on to say this has led to the remit of schools to now encompass notions of 'well-being and welfare' rather than just learning, with teachers expected to assess a child's 'emotional competence'.

Seemingly hand in hand with identity politics, she says self-reporting and the 'loosening of what clinically-recognised diagnosis means, have led to a huge rise in students presenting themselves as in need of special help to get through their university course.'

So we end up with the diagnosed cases of ADHD doubling to a million in the United Kingdom in a generation and the huge expansion of counsellors in schools.

As she puts it, 'Emotional interventions based on diminished subjectivity formalise and encourage dependence on external emotional support offered by state agencies and a growing work-force of mentors, life coaches, counsellors, psychologists and therapists.'

It's a short journey to see why, in a clip that went viral, a student at Yale in 2015 screamed and shouted at a lecturer, following a protest about Halloween costumes, the words, 'It's about creating a home here!'

Is there a link between this behaviour and the recent spate of old-people hatred brought to the fore in the UK's Brexit aftermath where 'young people' viewed 'old people' who voted 'Leave' as idiots who should basically just die?

In a recent Twitter exchange featuring Toby Young, when he said that a *Guardian* article claiming GCSEs were affecting kids' mental health was rubbish and that kids in other countries doing far harder exams (let alone previous generations) seemed to cope, he was met with comments from parents saying their kids have it tougher, and stress levels are much greater.

It's a wildly complex, subjective and clearly emotive subject, but most kids from previous generations recall little or no help from teachers, let alone parents, to accomplish good results. Doesn't make it right of course, but can we not talk about it?

What's more worrying is the almost rabid levels of glee from some of the parents. Again, like the child's suffering was a weird badge of honour. My child suffers more so 'ner'. Maybe a competitive sports day would have driven that feeling out.

As Suzanne Moore puts it, 'The issue, then, is not whether we prioritise pensioners over spoilt brats, but how to square respect or even basic care for older people with the insane fetishisation of childhood. Somewhere in the midst of this we must see how the links between the generations are unravelling.'[35]

So where *does* this end? As I've said, everything might be fine. And to be honest, as long as you parents give me the same respect I afford you, we should be OK. However, we've recently seen an apparent minority of students at colleges and university battling people who have been invited to speak at their campus and dare to hold different views to them. 'Safe space' is an oft-ridiculed term, but where did it come from? Originally intended to protect LGBT students, it's been to the gym since then, jacked itself up on performance enhancing drugs and got itself a little gang. It sounds a lot like the language of a child psychologist. Safe space. Time outs. Naughty step?

How about we reward students who do expose their minds to different views with lollipops? Worth a try?

The Charlie Zelenoff internet phenomenon is an interesting one. Charlie claims to be the greatest boxer in the world. This fascinating young man is at best a fantasist but is probably suffering from a delusion-based mental illness. His biggest claims to fame include sucker punching anyone he can, such as Floyd Mayweather Junior's sixty-year-old dad, before running away.[36]

Charlie comes across as a terrible coward – selecting people he sees as weaker than him or, more often than not, unaware he is about to sneakily punch them in the face.

Despite his only pro fight ending in him being disqualified (for continually spitting his gumshield out once he realised he was outmatched) this LA-born 'welterweight' continued to make outrageous claims of boxing prowess and heartfelt, yet somehow threatening, proclamations of love for Nicki Minaj and Kim Kardashian.

Labelled a troll and a lunatic by most, what's more interesting is Charlie's parents seem to be indulging and, worryingly, enabling him. At one point his father appears to be acting as his trainer / promoter.

Is Charlie's dad also mentally ill? Maybe the whole family are in some kind of collective delusion. Or does his dad just not want to disappoint his child? Maybe he wants to be his friend, no matter the cost? It seems that the latter is the most likely motive. Or perhaps he is, like so many parents, trying to cling onto some remnant of their own youth.

Our bar has got so low, our indoctrination so deep, that we don't seem to think it's peculiar when we see a grown adult reading Harry Potter. And there's no escape from the obsession; some tube announcements on the London Underground are now read out by a child who has managed to add being patronised to the already inhuman experience of commuting, and the infantilisation seems to reach every aspect of life with Sky News in the United Kingdom recently summing up local election results by attributing emojis to each political party.

Hope lies in children apparently, and so we must dream that Generation Z or the one that follows realises pretty quickly that mum and dad might be a pair of pathetic parasites who are not to be trusted and, like all good children, respect what they should and revolt against what came before them.

They'll have to navigate this climate carefully, and the backlash that has come from an assortment of 'red-pilled' 'heroes' who want a return to 'traditionalism' as a way of fighting political correctness. In their alternative Eden, these pasty-faced Beta males and females will have women walking barefoot and being the baby-making machines nature intended, while the men get to forage and protect while wearing those weird trainers with toes.

Philip Larkin was right; they'll see your corrosive cocooning of their experiences and marketing of their lives for your own social currency as a self-serving agenda that has damaged their chances to lead a successful and rewarding life.

The day will come when they reject you, and it will come with the click of a button or swipe of a screen. It will come with a single word. Blocked.

The end.

Acknowledgements

THANKS TO THE internet and all its wonders, and to the inspirational gaggle of talented people I interact with on the social media (though most of you are simply responsible for posting the various memes that have stopped me from finishing this book when I should have), you are the wind beneath my ROFLcopter.

To my friends whose approach to parenting helped me realise how annoying the bad ones are, thank you.

Particular thanks to 'my dearest piggy' Keith, and to Amanda, Nick, Nick, probably another Nick, Sophie, Howard, Daz, Loz and others for their help, advice and encouragement.

To my two cats Spook and Shiner for being weird.

To the ever-talented Delme for his artistic flare and a damn fine cover, thanks.

And to those parents who feel a kinship or even sympathy with aspects of what I have written, thanks, but most of all, this is for you. You must hate it more than anyone. Stay strong and be proud of what you achieve. You are literally responsible for the future. No pressure but don't mess this up.

And to G, thank you for being the most magnificent human being I know and a constant source of inspiration, love and support.

And finally, to my mum. Life made me a cynical twisted ratbag, but the good bits are all you.

References

1. The rise of childlessness / *The Economist* 27/7/2017 www.econo-mist.com/international/2017/07/27/the-rise-of-childlessness

2. How to ban newspapers and influence people / *The Spectator* 15/1/2018   blogs.spectator.co.uk/2018/01/virgin-trains-bungled-daily-mail-ban-is-a-warning-for-virtue-signallers/

3. Mothers are to blame for this child-obsessed society of ours / *The Guardian* 10/8/2008 www.theguardian.com/commentis-free/2008/aug/10/children.equality

4. Los Feliz Daycare @LosFelizDaycare Twitter 23/5/2019

5. Various sources including: Are Kids Too Fragile? / YouTube – ReasonTV 26/10/2017 www.youtube.com/watch?v=6-SrsJiq0AE

6. Free-Range Kids / Laura Skenazy www.freerangekids.com/book/

7. Gemma Collins has strangers offering to help her get pregnant after devastating fertility news on TOWIE / *Metro* 6/4/2017 metro.co.uk/2017/04/06/gemma-collins-has-strangers-offering-

to-help-her-get-pregnant-after-devastating-fertility-news-on-towie-6558091/

8. Onward 'Cheerful Warriors': Why Parents Are Unhappy / Parents.com   www.parents.com/parents-magazine/parents-perspective/onward-cheerful-warriors-why-parents-are-unhappy/

9. Children are the opium of the masses, says Rory Stewart / *The Telegraph* 21/10/2013 10 Paul Foot 'Baby on Board Comedy / YouTube 16/5/2013 www.youtube.com/watch?v=Qx5hralV4kA

10. Father loses damages claim over forged IVF signature / *The Guardian* 17/12/2018 www.theguardian.com/law/2018/dec/17/father-loses-damages-claim-over-forged-ivf-signature

11. Surrogacy and Gay Couples / New Feminism 2/6/2015 http://www.newfeminism.co/2015/06/surrogacy-and-gay-couples/

12. The Couple Having Four Babies by Two Surrogates / BBC Asian Network 28/10/2013 www.bbc.co.uk/news/uk-24670212

13. Various sources including: Why have so many people in prison spent time in care as children? / *The Conversation* 26/10/2016 the-conversation.com/why-have-so-many-people-in-prison-spent-time-in-care-as-children-66941 And Offending rates among children in care investigated / BBC 23/6/2015 www.bbc.co.uk/news/uk-33221247

14. Disposable Diapers Add Millions of Tons of Waste to Landfills Each Year, According to EPA Report / Cision 31/12/2016 www.prnewswire.com/news-releases/disposable-diapers-

add-millions-of-tons-of-waste-to-landfills-each-year-according-to-epa-report-300384344.html

15. Having children is one of the most destructive things you can do to the environment, say researchers / *The Independent* 12/7/2017 www.independent.co.uk/environment/children-carbon-foot-print-climate-change-damage-having-kids-research-a7837961.html

16. Not Dumb, Not Blonde: Dolly in Conversation by Dolly Parton, Randy Schmidt

17. There, I've Said It / Lucy Mangan *Stylist* magazine 1/5/2017

18. Mumsnet reveal the lengths that parents will go to for their kids primary school places / *Metro* 13/4/2018 metro.co.uk/2018/04/13/mumsnet-reveal-lengths-parents-will-go-kids-primary-school-places-7463857/

19. The rise of childlessness / *The Economist* 27/7/2017 www.economist.com/international/2017/07/27/the-rise-of-childlessness

20. Andre Leadsom 'motherhood' comments spark row / BBC (and others) 9/7/2016 www.bbc.co.uk/news/uk-politics-36752865

21. "I've got a wife and children": Owen Smith's Andrea Leadsom moment / NewStatesman 18/7/2016 www.newstatesman.com/politics/staggers/2016/07/i-ve-got-wife-and-children-owen-smith-s-andrea-leadsom-moment

22. Cameron Diaz: Women who don't want children fear being shunned' / *The Independent* 10/6/2009 www.independent.co.uk/news/people/news/cameron-diaz-women-who-dont-want-children-fear-being-shunned-1701458.html

23. Mobile phones are destroying family life – but it's the parents who are to blame, study claims / *Mirror* 24/4/2017 www.mirror.co.uk/tech/mobile-phones-destroying-family-life-10286970

24. Big Mouth Strikes Again / SimonPegg.net 19/5/2015 www.simon-pegg.net/2015/05/19/big-mouth-strikes-again/

25. We wouldn't feed our kids junk food. So why let them use emo-jis? / *The Spectator* 12/5/2018 www.spectator.co.uk/2018/05/we-wouldnt-feed-our-kids-junk-food-so-why-let-them-use-emojis/

26. Millenials 'set to be fattest generation ever' / SkyNews 26/2/2018 news.sky.com/story/millennials-on-course-to-be-fattest-genera-tion-ever-research-shows-11268322

27. Cancer Research, UK, links obesity to cancer with ads resembling cigarette packs / *Campaign* 2/7/2019 www.campaignlive.co.uk/article/cancer-research-uk-links-obesity-cancer-ads-resembling-cigarette-packs/1589767

28. Award-winning comedian accuses Cancer Research of 'fat-sham-ing' for launching campaign against obesity / *The Telegraph* 1/3/2018 www.telegraph.co.uk/news/2018/03/01/award-win-ning-comedian-accuses-cancer-research-fat-shaming-launching/

29. Are 'non-competitive sports days' really better for school kids? / *The Guardian* 9/7/2017 www.theguardian.com/education/shortcuts/2017/jul/09/are-non-competitive-sports-days-really-better-for-school-kids

30. No kids allowed: Is Britain becoming an anti-child society? / *The Telegraph* 31/8/2017 www.telegraph.co.uk/family/parenting/no-kids-allowed-is-britain-becoming-an-anti-child-society/

31. Pupils as young as four having panic attacks say teachers / BBC News 14/4/2017 www.bbc.co.uk/news/education-39589910

32. Half Hour of Heterodoxy / YouTube 5/7/2017 www.youtube.com/watch?v=bQ0fZffZFS8

33. Children 'vulnerable' by therapy culture / *The Telegraph* 16/11/2009 www.telegraph.co.uk/education/6583453/Children-left-vulnerable-by-therapy-culture.html

34. The worship of children brings only misery / *The Guardian* 23/10/2013 www.theguardian.com/commentisfree/2013/oct/23/worship-children-brings-misery-suzanne-moore

35. Various sources including: Who Is Charlie Zelenoff? / Handerick www.handerick.com/who-is-charlie-zelenoff/

OTHER SOURCES AND FURTHER READING

Free Range Kids www.freerangekids.com/
Mumsnet www.mumsnet.com/

For further information visit yourchildrenareboring.com

Sauce Materials

www.saucematerials.co.uk

Made in the USA
Las Vegas, NV
15 January 2021

15980985R00060